TOGETHER APART

Sara Miller McCune founded SAGE Publishing in 1965 to support the dissemination of usable knowledge and educate a global community. SAGE publishes more than 1000 journals and over 800 new books each year, spanning a wide range of subject areas. Our growing selection of library products includes archives, data, case studies and video. SAGE remains majority owned by our founder and after her lifetime will become owned by a charitable trust that secures the company's continued independence.

Los Angeles | London | New Delhi | Singapore | Washington DC | Melbourne

TOGETHER
APART
THE
PSYCHOLOGY
OF COVID-19

**JOLANDA JETTEN, STEPHEN D. REICHER,
S. ALEXANDER HASLAM AND TEGAN CRUWYS**

Los Angeles | London | New Delhi
Singapore | Washington DC | Melbourne

Los Angeles | London | New Delhi
Singapore | Washington DC | Melbourne

SAGE Publications Ltd
1 Oliver's Yard
55 City Road
London EC1Y 1SP

SAGE Publications Inc.
2455 Teller Road
Thousand Oaks, California 91320

SAGE Publications India Pvt Ltd
B 1/I 1 Mohan Cooperative Industrial Area
Mathura Road
New Delhi 110 044

SAGE Publications Asia-Pacific Pte Ltd
3 Church Street
#10-04 Samsung Hub
Singapore 049483

Editor: Amy Maher
Editorial assistant: Marc Barnard
Production editor: Imogen Roome
Copyeditor: Sarah Bury
Proofreader: Leigh C. Smithson
Indexer: Adam Pozner
Marketing manager: Camille Richmond
Cover design: Wendy Scott
Typeset by: C&M Digitals (P) Ltd, Chennai, India
Printed in the UK

Example citation:
Steffens, N. K. (2020). Compliance and followership. In J. Jetten, S. D. Reicher, S. A. Haslam, & T. Cruwys. *Together Apart: The Psychology of COVID-19*. London: Sage.

First published 2020

Library of Congress Control Number: 2020939186

British Library Cataloguing in Publication data

A catalogue record for this book is available from the British Library

ISBN 978-1-5297-5209-0

At SAGE we take sustainability seriously. Most of our products are printed in the UK using responsibly sourced papers and boards. When we print overseas we ensure sustainable papers are used as measured by the PREPS grading system. We undertake an annual audit to monitor our sustainability.

Contents

Author Biographies

This book provides a broad but integrated analysis of the psychology of COVID-19. The book is the product of the combined effort of four social psychologists: *Jolanda Jetten* (top left; Professor of Social Psychology and Australian Laureate Fellow at The University of Queensland), *Stephen (Steve) Reicher* (bottom left; Wardlaw Professor of Psychology at the University of St Andrews), *S. Alexander (Alex) Haslam* (top right; Professor of Psychology and Australian Laureate Fellow at The University of Queensland) and *Tegan Cruwys* (bottom right; Senior Research Fellow at The Australian National University).

What these four social psychologists have in common is that over the last decades their research has inspired, and has been inspired by, research and theory around the topic of social identity. In this, they have shown how the social identity approach helps us to understand processes as diverse as leadership, health, well-being, emergency behaviour, risk perception, stigma, inequality, stereotyping, collective action, crowd behaviour, intergroup violence, social cohesion and solidarity, populism, political rhetoric, obedience, and the psychology of tyranny.

Since the start of the COVID-19 pandemic, the authors have been advising a range of bodies on how to best support the COVID-19 response. They have provided input on topics including communications and messaging, adherence to lockdown and physical distancing, trust-building, leadership, public order, how to motivate people to download COVID-19 tracing apps, and the mental health impact of physical distancing measures. They have advised the UK Government and the Scottish Government, the UK police force, and the Australian Government's Behavioural Economics Team (BETA) in the Department of the Prime Minster and Cabinet. They have also been members of a number of bodies and task forces, including the G08 Australian Roadmap to Recovery, the Australian Broadcasting Corporation's COVID Monitor project, the British Psychological Society COVID Coordinating Group, and the Rapid Response Information Forum on COVID-19 tracing in Australia. In this engagement with policy makers and governments it has become clear how psychological theory, and the social identity approach in particular, can help us better understand, and respond to, the COVID-19 crisis. This book is an attempt to put what they and their colleagues have been talking about over the past three months into print, so that insights from the social identity approach can contribute to public debate about the most significant world event of our lifetimes.

Contributors

Section B

Niklas K. Steffens, The University of Queensland

Frank Mols, The University of Queensland

Matthew J. Hornsey, The University of Queensland

Section C

Katharine H. Greenaway, University of Melbourne

Sarah V. Bentley, The University of Queensland

Catherine Haslam, The University of Queensland

Orla Muldoon, University of Limerick

Section D

Fergus Neville, University of St Andrews

John Drury, University of Sussex

Selin Tekin Guven, University of Sussex

Evangelos Ntontis, Canterbury Christ Church University

Carolina Rocha, University of St Andrews

Holly Carter, Public Health England

Dale Weston, Public Health England

Richard Amlôt, Public Health England

Clifford Stott, Keele University

Matt Radburn, Keele University

Section E

Charlie R. Crimston, The University of Queensland

Hema Preya Selvanathan, The University of Queensland

Yuen J. Huo, University of California, Los Angeles

John F. Dovidio, Yale University

Elif G. Ikizer, University of Wisconsin-Green Bay

Jonas R. Kunst, University of Oslo

Aharon Levy, Yale University

Acknowledgements

The idea for this book emerged in early March 2020 when it became clear that COVID-19 was going to affect the lives of a large proportion of people on our planet in profound ways. Starting from the premise that an effective response to the pandemic depends upon people coming together and supporting each other as members of a common community, the aim of this book is to use social identity theorising to provide a comprehensive and integrated analysis of the psychology of COVID-19. This is a big task and it is not one we could have undertaken alone. Accordingly, as the list of contributors above indicates, we needed to approach a large number of researchers at the forefront of social identity theorising to help us develop and flesh out this analysis. The result is a book that is a hybrid between a monograph and an edited book. Although this is an unusual format, we believe that this structure allows us to showcase the power and excitement not only of social identity research but also of the collective processes this research involves. We hope you agree.

The way this book developed was also somewhat unusual. First, we not only experienced considerable time pressure to write the book within the time frame we set ourselves (less than two months), but also, given the rapidly evolving nature of the COVID-19 crisis, we needed to re-evaluate and re-think our analysis on an almost daily basis. We were studying a phenomenon that had not yet ended. Second, we wrote this book while self-isolating at home. Even though we are normally spread across the world in three different cities, and even though writing a book together would always have meant being physically distant, this somehow felt different. This was perhaps because it is the first time that we ourselves were not only researchers, but also participants and thus at the heart of the thing we were studying. Indeed, because we are still in the midst of the COVID-19 crisis, it is very likely that aspects of our analysis will be somewhat outdated and incomplete by the time the book appears, and readers should be mindful of this. Nevertheless, we are confident that much of the book's content has enduring relevance – and indeed it was this that really motivated us to produce it.

What is clear is that both the time pressure and the immersion in the focus of study made this a unique book to write. In order to meet the deadline and to understand the daily unfolding dynamics world-wide, regular Zoom meetings and brainstorm sessions were essential, not just to coordinate the writing, but also to get a grip on the reality that was taking shape around us. The truly collaborative nature of this project hopefully shines through in terms of the level of integration across sections and chapters. This is a project built around partnerships, not personalities, and authorship (of both the book and the chapters) should be understood as a reflection of shared social identities ('we-ness'), not of disconnected personal identities ('me-ness').

In the same spirit we would also like to draw attention to others who were invaluable in this collective endeavour. In particular, we are grateful to the team at SAGE, led by Amy Maher, who were enthusiastic about our plans from the start and have worked tirelessly to facilitate a rapid publication of this book. Thank you too to Christine McCoy and Joe Sheahan for their excellent support in proof reading and reference checking – all under a fair amount of time pressure. We would also like to thank the funding bodies, without whom much of the research that forms the basis of this book would not have been possible. Principal among these are the Australian Research Council, the National Health and Medical Research Council in Australia, as well as our respective universities: The University of Queensland, the University of St Andrews, and The Australian National University. It is our hope that this book will form a solid foundation on which future analysis, intervention and policy relating to the COVID-19 crisis can be built, and that it can help pave the way for a future together.

Jolanda Jetten, Steve Reicher, Alex Haslam, Tegan Cruwys
May 29, 2010

Foreword

Social distancing, really? When international organisations and the media initially reported about the spread of a new deadly virus spotted in China, governments took some time to react. As the tsunami of contaminations started to threaten other parts of the world, epidemiologists informed the public that, along with scrupulous hand hygiene, so-called social distancing was the weapon 'par excellence' in order to deal with a pandemic. Many social and behavioural scientists frowned and commented on the lessons of research stressing the critical role of social relations, especially when people face challenging events. As the various contributions in this book make clear, of all terms, 'social distancing' is probably as inappropriate as one can get. To be sure, keeping a distance between individuals and cutting society down into very small groups (families and work teams) that have no physical contact with each other offers an efficient means to slow down the spread of the virus. But from the perspective of social psychology in particular, what is key in times of hardship – and the COVID pandemic surely qualifies as a prime instance of a large-scale disaster – is to work towards more 'social bonding' between people.

By the end of February, the number of cases had increased rapidly in Italy and elsewhere in Europe, and keeping the deadly virus at bay quickly became *the* common cause. Given the dearth of information about the evolution of the illness and its associated symptoms, all citizens were potential victims and the decision of most governments was to ask people to retreat securely into their homes. But how can you shut down thriving societies in an instant? How can you convince thousands of businesses to close? How can you get people not to go to work, children not to see their schoolmates, friends not to organise parties, shoppers not to go to malls, fans not to attend sporting events or music festivals? Would people resist sudden restrictions of their freedom of movement? Would they disregard the recommendations, eventually jeopardising the capacity of the health systems? Although contemporary political gospel has it that individual rationality and self-interest guide human behaviour, the imminence and size of the danger changed things radically. A number of leaders did not take long to understand that the success of a radical lockdown would rest on their ability to create a sense of collective identity, connecting and coordinating citizens under one common banner. Political figures from various strands of the ideological spectrum changed gears entirely and came to realise that only creating shared identity would allow bringing millions of peoples to stay home willingly and to embrace the preventive measures with faith. And it worked …

Over the course of the last couple of months and in every single aspect of the fight against the pandemic, it has become clear that one should approach the issue in ways that stress the social over the individual, reinforce the sense of belonging as opposed to a feeling of independence, and acknowledge common identity in contrast to uniqueness. To be sure, it is individuals who carry the disease, contaminate others, and, in some cases, die. It is individuals who buy an excess of toilet paper, who prove reluctant to wear a mask because they fear ridicule or neglect to wash their hands for the twentieth time upon entering their workplace. And it is also individuals who stay inside in spite of the sunny weather, who work remotely and endure the burden of schooling their children, who run to the supermarket for their elderly neighbour on the second floor. But what needs to be understood is that all these behaviours follow from perceptions, emotions, and decisions eminently shaped by social forces. More often than not, people self-define in terms of significant memberships, and all the more so when they feel uncertain. Behaviours are not the product of isolated souls, but emerge in a socially meaningful context, a context in which people make up their minds and undergo emotional experiences as part of larger entities.

The impressive number of research efforts assembled in the present contribution and generally stimulated by the so-called social identity approach makes one thing very clear: nurturing the social in people's minds is not the problem but it is the solution. By capitalising on appropriate social identities, often at the national level, group leaders can work and make people become more sensitive to specific messages. This is because the persuasiveness of a communication rests on the extent to which the audience sees the source as 'one of us'. By ensuring that people continue to feel connected with fellow members of significant social entities, one can avoid the perils of social isolation and lack of social support, two prime causes of deteriorating health and premature death. It is thus crucial that citizens are provided with opportunities to feel emotional support. This can take the form of close relatives talking over the phone or organising drinks over social media, of heretofore-unknown neighbours dropping a warm note under the door. People also need to feel 'in touch', as when they see others applaud on their balcony to celebrate the dedication of nurses and doctors working in intensive care units. By promoting selected ways of delineating the social landscape, it is possible to create a sense of collective identity that then feeds into collective action. Indeed, in so many ways, fighting COVID-19 becomes a prototypical form of collective action. And research shows that successful collective action rests on the definition of a clearly defined common cause, hangs on a sense of collective efficacy, and capitalises on the energy flowing from collective emotions.

This means that, more than ever, the current events require so-called 'entrepreneurs of identity'. There is a need for people who emphasise the shared cause while acknowledging different perspectives in order to keep everybody aboard. There is a need for people who communicate clearly about those behaviours that ought to become the norm, who are credible as they convey their trust in the population's ability to comply, and who are transparent about progress but also setbacks. There is a need for people who make room for emotional experiences, signifying that, while fear is understandable and may even help increase vigilance, empathy and hope are key to getting us all through. Finally, by attuning communication to different groups in society, and even more so by addressing the specific consequences of the pandemic for different portions of the population, one should be able to prevent the dislocation of the collective.

The message is clear: social distancing is a real misnomer. While physical distance undoubtedly contributes to preventing contamination, this book provides ample evidence that the vital feature of any successful action against the virus is to capitalise on shared identity and group-based emotions, in short, on a common definition of 'who we are'. Only by embracing such a perspective can one hope to minimise the subjective costs of individual sacrifices and promote the aspiration for collective dividends that will eventually benefit all parties involved. In sum, the key to addressing large-scale crises such as the outbreak of COVID-19 resides in our ability to stay away from individualistic interpretations of the events and to acknowledge the fact that what truly defines human beings is their inherent disposition for social bonding.

These are the various messages that this book communicates and consolidates. And this is why, in this most challenging of times, this book is so important.

Vincent Yzerbyt

Professor of Psychology, Université catholique de Louvain,
Louvain-la-Neuve

Former President, European Association of Social Psychology

Advisor for the Crisis Centre of the Belgian Federal Government

SECTION

A SETTING THE SCENE

1

The Need for a Social Identity Analysis of COVID-19

As we write, at the start of May 2020, 4 million people have been infected with COVID-19, over a quarter of a million have died, and more than a third of the entire population of the planet is under some form of restriction of movement. It is the biggest health emergency of our generation. And yet, unless or until a vaccine is developed, or we discover medicines to treat the virus, our means of controlling the spread of infection depend on behavioural changes and hence upon human psychology.

This is most obvious in the case of lockdown. While it is all very well to tell people that they must stay at home in order to flatten the curve of infection, the effectiveness of the policy depends on whether or not they do. Just how sensitive the curve is to even minor changes in compliance is made clear by Figure 1, which was created at the end of March by Mark Woolhouse – one of the epidemiologists advising the UK government. As this graph shows, a fully compliant population could reduce the proportion of those infected at the end of a three-week lockdown by a factor of 10: from 4.1% to under 0.4%. In Britain, this would amount to a vast difference in infection numbers – from approximately 2.75 million to 270,000 people infected. Similar calculations around the world have inspired many government-led campaigns to encourage people to '*Stay at Home and Save Lives*'. Behaviour, then, is clearly critical. Indeed, all we can do to control the virus right now is get people to behave appropriately – to 'do the right thing'.

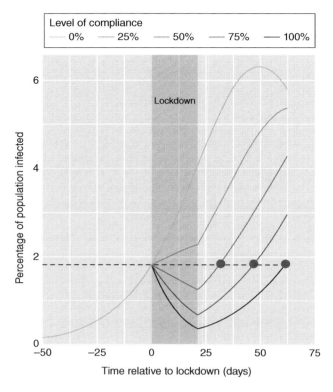

Figure 1 Sensitivity of the COVID-19 infection curve to different levels of compliance

A sceptic might retort that this is a matter of picking low-hanging fruit. Of course, the lockdown is a matter of changing what people do. But one of its key aims is to give us time to prepare and reduce the levels of infection so that they can then be dealt with by other types of intervention. This sceptic's argument suggests that as the days of lockdown are numbered, so too is the relevance of behaviour and psychology to controlling COVID-19. To assess the validity of this retort, let us consider two of the interventions that have been most discussed in recent weeks: one is the wearing of face masks; the other is the use of 'Test, Trace, Isolate' (TTI). In other words, find out who is infected, find out who they have been in contact with, isolate those people so they cannot infect others and, in that way, nip the spread in the bud.

The issue around face masks seems very simple. The masks available to the public probably do not prevent a tiny virus getting through and infecting you. But they do stop you breathing, coughing and spluttering the virus over others if you are infected. Overall, it seems a no-brainer: wear masks and reduce the virus spread. Where is the psychology in that?

It is worth starting off by making a small but important distinction. By itself, a mask does not stop anything. It is wearing masks that makes the difference. And wearing masks is a behaviour. Then, just as with the behaviour of staying at home, the question is will people do it or not? Furthermore, the literature on the effectiveness of mask wearing to prevent infection provides rather mixed results. If you wear them properly and dispose of them carefully, they probably have a modestly positive effect (Greenhalgh, Schmid, Czypionka, Bassler, & Gruer, 2020). But people do not wear them properly. They fit them badly, they lift them to speak, they touch them, they leave them lying on surfaces, and they casually toss them aside. And if they do too much of this, masks may do more harm than good. There are very few high-quality studies of how people actually use masks in everyday settings. But such behavioural investigation is crucial before we can really determine whether masks are worthwhile.

And then there are all the impacts of mask wearing that go beyond the physical impact of the mask. Will they cut us off from others, dehumanise us, further isolate us from other people even when we venture out of our homes? Will they signal danger, increase anxiety, and serve as a further detriment to mental health at a time when people are already scared and anxious not only of getting ill and dying, but also of the economic and political hardship that the pandemic is causing? Will they cause social division and even conflict between those who do and do not wear masks, so that some people accuse others of acting recklessly and foolishly? Conversely, in so far as masks serve to protect others from us rather than us from others, will wearing them create positive social norms? Will masks serve as a public sign that people are acting for the common good and hence strengthen impulses towards kindness and compassion? These questions are just some of the many ways in which the impact of masks on the trajectory of COVID-19 is critically dependent on psychological considerations.

Similar points can be made about 'Test, Trace, Isolate'. Briefly, the strategy is totally dependent on people's willingness to be tested, to be tracked, and then to isolate themselves. And hence compliance is as important here as it is with lockdown and with mask wearing. The issue of tracking is particularly problematic. In many countries, people are being asked to download an app onto their phones that will continuously collect data about their proximity to others (or, rather, to others' phones). Then, if someone tests positive, this information can be used by health agencies to trace the people with whom they have had contact. But will enough people comply to make the system work? Will they be happy with a state agency having such detailed information about their social interactions? In particular, will groups who are more antagonistic to authority willingly submit themselves to this type of 'Big Brother' surveillance?

What these examples make clear is that there are a great many psychological issues that shape the impact (for good and for ill) of every measure that governments around the world are contemplating or using to deal with the pandemic. And just as the pandemic itself is unique in our lifetimes, so too we see for the first time a realisation by governments (and by society more widely) that it needs to harness psychology as a key element in strategies to defeat COVID-19. Moreover, and this really is new, governments are seeing psychology not only as relevant to individual-level outcomes (e.g., the effects of the pandemic on mental health), but also as integral to societal-level outcomes (e.g., the maintenance of social cohesion or conversely the development of public disorder).

However, it is not enough to understand that we need psychology as a core part of efforts against COVID-19. It is also important to understand what *sort* of psychology helps or hinders in those efforts.

We need a psychological analysis that recognises people are the solution not the problem

Both within and beyond the academic discipline of psychology, there is a long-standing and influential tradition that views people as mentally frail, beset by biases, and unable to deal with uncertainty, complexity or stress – and therefore prone to unravel completely in a crisis. This kind of psychology holds that when the going gets tough, the people panic (an idea we will examine in more detail in Sections B and D). When the crisis hits, the people become part of the problem. So, they need to be shielded from harsh truths, and shepherded by a paternalistic government who must factor in the frailty of the masses when deciding what forms of disaster management are viable.

We have seen various aspects of this 'frailty' tradition in responses to COVID-19. As the dangers posed by the virus began to become clear, the media was full of stories of 'panic buying'. We were warned that people did not have the willpower to sustain prolonged restrictions and that 'behavioural fatigue' would set in. And after the lockdown was imposed, the media shifted their attention to so-called 'covidiots' who were flouting regulations, flocking to outdoor spaces, and organising indoor parties.

This lack of trust in the psychology of the people had important practical implications (Reicher, 2020). At worst, it was used to undermine medical recommendations as to what measures were needed to control infection. In many countries, the concept of 'behavioural fatigue' was notoriously invoked to justify a delay in lockdown. It also encouraged a punitive response towards those who failed to adhere to lockdown regulations. The notion that such non-adherence (e.g., going to the park) was the product of psychological weakness or malevolence led to threats of both individual punishment (imposing fines) and collective punishment (closing down the parks).

There are many problems with such an approach. The first is that it is contradicted by what actually happened. In many ways, the headline story of COVID-19 is not the weakness but the strength of the people. Breaking the rules tends to make better headlines than observing the rules, and so stories of people plundering supermarket shelves for toilet rolls or flouting lockdown have filled the front pages (e.g., see Figure 4 in Chapter 4). Nonetheless, the overall figures show that very few people stockpiled scarce commodities. Equally, the great majority observed restrictions (indeed, far more than authorities in many countries had expected). And it was not easy. One analysis shows that, of the 92% of the UK population supporting lockdown, nearly half (44%) were suffering hardship as a result of the lockdown. It is no hyperbole to say that their behaviour has been heroic.

What is more, when people did violate the lockdown, this had less to do with psychological frailties than with practical difficulties. One particularly telling study showed that the poorest people in Britain were three times more likely than the most affluent to go out to work (Bibby, Everest, & Abbs, 2020; Smith, 2020b). But crucially, there was no difference in their psychological motivation to stay at home. It was simply that they needed to go to work to put food on the table.

The implication here is that, when attempting to increase adherence, waving a big stick at people generally misses the point. Instead of seeking to enforce lockdown on an unwilling population, the priority must be to enable people to do what they actually want to do. If they leave home from economic necessity, then provide the funding that allows them to stay in. If they leave home to exercise (as they are allowed to do in many countries) and inadvertently find themselves in crowded parks, then make available more green space (such as golf courses and playing fields) so they can keep a safe distance.

It is worth dwelling on this point for a moment, for it illustrates another central theme of this book – the role of social inequalities in this crisis and the impact of this crisis on social inequalities. The following statement was made by an inhabitant of the Paris suburb of Clichy-sous-Bois (a suburb with a high proportion of residents of North African descent), but could be from almost anywhere:

> People are trying to respect the lockdown, but what do you do if you're
> a family of five or more in a small apartment on the 15th floor? How do
> you keep children in? How do you feed them when the markets where
> you buy cheap fruit and vegetables have closed and you can't afford
> supermarkets? How can families whose children normally eat in school
> canteens now make three meals a day?

This makes the point that poverty places significant demands on people and these demands have limited their ability to comply with lockdown regulations (a point we develop further in Section E). Moreover, if these demands led people to venture out, the French state intervened with severe sanctions. In the first 16 days of lockdown alone the police carried out 5.8 million controls and issued 359,000 fines (FR24 News, 2020). Little surprise that suburbs like Clichy-sous-Bois were the origin of rioting, which then spread across France.

This takes us to the second main problem with the 'psychological frailty' perspective. It is not just wrong to see people as the problem in a crisis, it is also dangerous. On the one hand, it leads policy makers to look to psychology as the basis of problems of adherence and so ignores the real practical problems people face (much like the famous story of the British guns in Singapore pointing out to sea and thereby ignoring the fact that the real threat came from the land). On the other hand, and potentially even more seriously, a punitive approach may actually corrode the public's motivation to accept measures put in place by the authorities, breed resistance, and even lead to social disorder.

But the most important problem with the 'psychological frailty' approach is not the problems it causes, so much as the opportunities that it misses. For it is not just that the public proved very willing to comply with what they were told by the authorities. Rather, the public have played a highly active role in this pandemic. In many countries, they pushed governments into taking action, both to implement policies like lockdown and to provide the packages of support to make adherence possible. Moreover, across the globe, the mutual self-help shown at neighbour, street, community and national levels has been overwhelming. For instance, in the Netherlands, COVID-related volunteering has been at levels not seen since the North Sea flood of 1953 (van Dijke, 2020). And this is only the tip of the iceberg. In many countries, formal groups have been supplemented by countless individual acts of kindness to erstwhile strangers: putting notes offering help through the door, baking cakes, delivering shopping, and much else besides.

In so many ways, then, the public have not been the problem but a key part of the solution in this pandemic (Levy, 2020). They have not been a source of frailty but of resilience. Indeed, arguably, their response has been the most precious resource available in combatting COVID-19. The role of governments should be to support and enlist this public resilience. As we discuss further in Section B, the 'frailty' perspective encourages governments to ignore or even to suppress community solidarity and resilience – an error of tragic proportions. As a counterpoint to this, what we therefore need is a psychological perspective which addresses the roots of such resilience and which can therefore help us to understand how it can be developed, nurtured and sustained.

At one level, the solution to this is very simple. It requires recognition that resilience is more than a personal quality located inside particular people. It is also a *collective* quality that develops between people (Williams et al., 2019). It arises when people come together as a group, when they come to see others as a source of support rather than as competitors who stand in their way (Yzerbyt & Phalet, 2020). However, in order to reach this simple conclusion, we must sweep away a century of anti-collectivism which regards people coming together in groups as a source of deep anxiety and hostility.

We need to get our heads around the 'we' concept

Another consensus that has developed both inside and outside the discipline of psychology, and in much of social science, is that individuals are rational and good, while groups are irrational and bad. Indeed, rationality has generally been understood as the enlightened pursuit of individual self-interest (particularly in economics; but for a critique see Akerlof & Kranton, 2010). From this perspective, becoming part of a group is a process of subversion and loss: as we become part of the mass, we lose our sense of self, we lose our capacity to reason, we shed our moral compass, we lack agency and become like sheep, helplessly following the herd. Fine upstanding citizens morph into a mindless mob. Sensible people become victims of groupthink. Thinkers become zombies. According to this model, if you want optimal outcomes, the best advice you can give people (and society) is to stand alone and apart from the group.

We will critique this analysis further in Sections B and D, but already we can see where this logic takes us in the midst of a pandemic. Audrey Whitlock was one of the leaders of the anti-lockdown protests in North Carolina. The lockdown, she argued, was an act of tyranny from central government, and stood in contradiction to the fundamental freedoms guaranteed to her under the US constitution (Owen, 2020). Audrey became infected with COVID-19, at which point she then argued that the requirement to quarantine herself was a further denial of her rights to go out, to mingle with others, and to join further protests. In this way, her consistent and determined pursuit of her individual rights increased the probability of infection spread and compromised the safety of the community as a whole. As long as Audrey Whitlock and others frame COVID-19 as a 'me' thing, this pandemic will be longer, deeper and deadlier.

Fixating on the individual 'me' is therefore a way of thinking – and a way of acting – which many have recognised as profoundly limiting in a pandemic. As New York's Governor, Andrew Cuomo, put it:

> Yeah it's your life do whatever you want, but you are now responsible for my life…. We started saying, 'It's not about me it's about *we*.' Get your head around the we concept. It's not all about you. It's about me too. It's about we. (Slattery, 2020)

Now, in many ways, we could stop here. For Cuomo's words are hard to improve upon as a statement of the core theme of this book. COVID-19 is not about me, it is about we. If you respond on the basis of me, then everyone is in trouble. If you respond on the basis of we, then the future is far brighter. To make the point, let us reflect on some examples.

Most people's sense of personal risk of succumbing to COVID-19 is rather low, particularly among younger groups (in March 2020 the World Heath Organization estimated that while 3% of people who contract the virus will die, the mortality rate is far higher for older people; Fink, 2020). So, if people were making decisions only in terms of what happens to them personally, many might conclude that it is not worth abiding by lockdown, and adherence rates would be much lower – possibly around 25%. But most people are not behaving in 'me' terms. In fact, one's sense of personal risk barely affects adherence to lockdown at all. Rather, according to data we have collected from nearly 6,000 respondents across 11 countries, what best predicts adherence is a sense of 'we are all in it together and we all need to come out of it together' (Jetten, Bentley, et al., 2020). That is, it is thinking in terms of 'we' that leads people to behave in the ways that are necessary to control COVID-19. This raises the issue of how to develop a sense of 'we-ness' and, in particular, how leadership can encourage a collective mindset. This is a key issue that we address in Section B.

But thinking in group terms is important not only in determining whether we adhere to lockdown and other such measures. It also determines how well we cope. So while physically isolating ourselves from other people has been necessary in order to limit infections and thereby preserve our physical health, this social isolation also has the potential to compromise both physical and mental health. A large body of work has shown that being part of groups is a powerful prophylactic against such conditions. Feeling part of a group, and having a sense that others are there to support you when you need them, reduces anxiety and stress, and thereby improves not only mental but also physical health (Haslam, Jetten, Cruwys, Dingle, & Haslam, 2018). The question that then arises is how can we build such a sense of 'we-ness', of social connectedness, even when we are distanced from each other? How can we keep people together when they are apart? That is one of the great challenges of this pandemic (which is why we referenced it in the title of the book). We address this question in Section C.

One more example of why 'we-thinking' is so important concerns the dynamics of solidarity and citizenship. In a disaster of any size, and certainly one as enveloping as this pandemic, the public sector simply lacks the capacity to deal with everyone's needs. There are not enough police, care workers or community nurses to look after everyone who needs shopping to be done, medicine to be delivered, or just to be checked in on to see if they are coping. We have already referred to the flowering of different forms of mutual aid that have emerged to fill the gap. But clearly this flowering is dependent on people thinking in communal rather than personal terms, and therefore being as concerned with the needs of other members of the community as with their own needs. To cite Anna Vickerstaff, one of the founders of the UK's mutual aid national network, 'we set this network up because we want to make sure that no one in our communities is being left to face this crisis alone'. These questions of collective action and collective solidarity around COVID-19 – how it develops, how it can be nurtured, why it breaks down, and with what consequences – are the focus of Section D.

Yet while we see many examples of groups at their best in a crisis, as we will see in Section E, we equally see many examples of groups at their worst. This is no less true in pandemics. During the Black Death, for instance, over 500 Jewish communities were destroyed across Europe. In one single day, St Valentine's day 1349, some 2,000 Jews were burnt to death. In many other cities, including Frankfurt-am-Main and Cologne, the entire Jewish population was destroyed (Cohn, 2007). In the current crisis we are also witnessing outbreaks of collective hatred. In India, for instance, Muslims have been blamed for spreading the disease – so-called 'Corona-Jihadism'. The novelist Arundhati Roy (2020a) has argued that 'we are suffering, not just from COVID, but from a crisis of hatred, from a crisis of hunger'. Her words are of relevance to many countries. Indeed, the Head of the United Nations, António Guterres, described the pandemic as unleashing 'a tsunami of hate and xenophobia, scapegoating and scaremongering' (Hudson, 2020).

This raises two final questions. The first is what determines the passage from a community united in compassion to communities divided by hate? As the question implies, this is not a matter of groups or not groups, but rather of how we draw group boundaries and define group cultures. It is a question of whether the 'we' includes all sectors of the community – minorities and majorities alike – or whether our community is divided into a 'we' and a 'they', and also whether 'they' are represented as a threat to our very survival. Are 'the Jews' polluting 'our' wells? Are 'the Muslims' using the infection as a weapon? And where, then, do these constructions of groups and intergroup relations come from?

The second question is how do the fault lines in society – between rich and poor, between ethnic minorities and majorities, between the precarious and the comfortable – affect what happens in the pandemic, and how does the pandemic impact those fault lines? As well as what happens to individuals, a crucial issue concerning COVID-19 is what it will do to our society and to the relations between groups within it. This is a key topic that we address in Section E.

Summing up

By now, hopefully we have persuaded you of three things. First, that the COVID-19 pandemic is as much about psychology as biology, and hence that, if we are to deal with the pandemic effectively, it is as important for us to understand how people behave as it is to understand how the virus behaves.

Second, the pandemic is about group psychology in particular. People are predominantly acting as members of a community and for the interests of their community; to the extent that they do so, we are likely to come out from these dark days in better shape. However, we must be particularly vigilant about the ways in which the group is defined. If we slip from 'we-thinking' to 'we-and-they-thinking', then all of us are in deep trouble.

Third, we urgently need a framework for understanding how people come to form groups, how they behave in groups, the consequences of being in groups, and the ways in which the boundaries of groups come to be drawn more or less conclusively. The social identity approach will help us to do all of these things. As such, the next chapter of this section will spell out some of its key principles.

2

A Social Identity Analysis
of COVID-19

Plague was the concern of all of us.... Thus, for example, a feeling
normally as *individual* as the ache of separation from those one loves
suddenly became a feeling in which all *shared alike* and – together with
fear – the greatest affliction of the long period of exile that lay ahead.
(Camus, *The Plague*, 1947, p. 61, emphasis added)

As Albert Camus tells it in *The Plague*, as soon as contagious disease swept
through the Algerian city of Oran and the city went into lockdown, the behaviour
of the residents changed. Emotions that had previously been experienced indi-
vidually became emotions shared by all. Likewise, if we are trying to understand
responses to a challenge where (at least potentially) 'we are all in this together',
we need a theoretical analysis that helps us to get to grips with the nature of that
shared and collective experience. Above all else, then, this is what this book seeks
to provide.

The social identity approach (consisting of *social identity theory*; Tajfel &
Turner, 1979, and its extension *self-categorization theory*; Turner, Hogg, Oakes,
Reicher, & Wetherell, 1987; Turner, Oakes, Haslam, & McGarty, 1994) is well
suited to this task. In particular, as we outline below, this theoretical framework
provides a parsimonious explanation for many of the COVID-19 puzzles that we
identified in Chapter 1: how the virus has changed the way we look at ourselves
and others, as well as how it has changed our relationship to the world and our
sense of what we value in it. Fundamentally, what we see here is that COVID-19
has changed our notions of 'self' and associated calculations of 'interest', so that

these are more inclusive of others. More particularly, whether we define ourselves as 'us' – and if so, who is included in that definition, becomes critical to our social and health-related behaviour. But before delving into such matters, it will be helpful to consider where the social identity approach started and what exactly it is.

Writing in the early 1970s, Henri Tajfel defined social identity as 'the individual's knowledge that he [or she] belongs to certain social groups together with some emotional and value significance to him [or her] of this group membership' (1972, p. 31). In other words, social identity refers to *group membership*, which serves to define a person's sense of 'who they are' in a particular social context. In contrast, *personal identity* refers to a person's sense of their individuality (e.g., their idiosyncratic abilities and tastes; Turner, 1982). Practically speaking, this means that when people see themselves in terms of their social identity, they self-define in terms of 'we' rather than in terms of 'I'. It also means that when people act in terms of their social identity, they interact with others on the basis of an identity that they either share (as 'us' ingroup members) or do not share (as 'us' ingroup members versus 'them' outgroup members).

Why would this distinction between personal and social identity matter in the context of responses to COVID-19? As we noted in Chapter 1, one important reason is that during the pandemic many of the behaviours engaged in can be seen as motivated much more by people's social identity than by their personal identity.

To give an example, if a young woman, Sophie, were to assess her situation purely in terms of her personal identity, it would be hard to understand why she would engage in physical distancing and stop having face-to-face get-togethers with her friends. Why would she stay at home when she is personally in a very low-risk group? Indeed, even if she were to become infected, statistically speaking, her chance of survival would be very high. To understand Sophie's behaviour, we need to look at the groups and categories to which she belongs. When we do, we can see that she stays at home because she identifies with her family, friendship groups, workplace, community, and country, and these groups all endorse a norm of 'staying home'. In other words, when we look at her social identities – the groups to which she belongs and identifies with and the groups whose destiny she shares – the reasons for Sophie's choices become clearer. Indeed, this examination makes it clear that her behaviour is determined not by a concern about becoming personally infected with the virus, but by a desire to protect other members of the groups to which she belongs. This sentiment is echoed by Camus in *The Plague*, where he observes:

> No longer were there individual destinies; only a collective destiny, made of plague and emotions shared by all. (Camus, 1947, p. 161)

Moreover, it is not just that responses to COVID-19 typically involve considerations that are relevant to 'us' rather than 'me'; it is also clear that effectively combatting the virus (whether reducing its spread or mitigating its negative consequences) requires a focus on the group and not the individual. This is an observation that many leaders have made. For example, Magnus Berntsson, the President of the Assembly of European Regions, remarked:

> It is only through cooperation that we can successfully battle this virus and deal with its long-term societal and economic effects. Nationalist and protectionist strategies will not succeed against an 'enemy' that does not respect borders. Coordination, cooperation, sharing of best practices and solidarity are needed now more than ever. (Assembly of European Regions, 2020)

The social identity approach is well placed to tackle the challenge of understanding how collective-level solidarity and cooperation can be achieved. In the remainder of this chapter, we outline the key premises of the social identity approach that are relevant to the psychology of COVID-19. In this, our main objectives are (a) to map out the forces that *determine* how people are able to act as group members rather than as individuals, and (b) to understand what the distinctive psychological and behavioural *consequences* of acting in terms of social identity are. In other words, what leads us to see ourselves as members of a given community (e.g., as 'Oranians under siege') and how does this change what we think, feel, and do?

We know who we are (and what to do) by comparing 'us' with 'them'

The above observations give an initial sense of why social identity – a sense of 'us-ness' – is so important for the psychology of COVID-19. But when do we see ourselves as one 'us' rather than many 'I's? And how do we know exactly who and what 'us' is?

Some initial answers to these questions were provided by a series of laboratory studies that Tajfel and colleagues conducted in the early 1970s – the so-called 'minimal group' studies (Tajfel, Billig, Bundy, & Flament, 1971). The participants in these studies were assigned to groups on the basis of ostensibly trivial criteria, such as their preference for the abstract painters Klee or Kandinsky. After this, they had to award points (signifying small amounts of money) to an anonymous member of their own group and to an anonymous member of the other group. The participants were never able to allocate money to themselves, so this

ruled out self-interest and personal economic gain as determinants of their alloca-
tion behaviour. All they knew was that they were allocating money either to 'us'
(without benefiting from that personally) or to 'them'.

The robust finding that emerged from these studies was that even these most
minimal of conditions were sufficient to encourage group behaviour. In particular,
participants tended to award more points to a person from their ingroup ('us') than
to a member of the outgroup ('them'). Tajfel and Turner (1979) explained these
findings by arguing that acting as group members (i.e., in terms of a social identity
as a member of the Klee group) helped to 'create and define the individual's place
in society' (pp. 40–41). More generally, they argued that often we only know who
'we' are by knowing who we are *not*. As Tajfel put it:

> Distinction from the 'other' category [e.g., the Kandinsky group] *pro-
> vided an identity for their own group*, and thus some kind of meaning to
> an otherwise empty situation. (1972, pp. 39–40, emphasis added)

This observation provided a platform for two theoretical principles which form
the core of *social identity theory*. First, groups define their place and standing in
the social world through *comparisons with other relevant groups*, and second, the
outcome of that social comparison is important because group members strive for
a sense of social identity that is *positive*, *distinct* and *enduring* (Tajfel & Turner,
1979). In other words, we want 'us' to be better than, different from and more
durable than 'them'.

There is plenty of evidence of these motivations at work in the context of
COVID-19. In particular, in trying to determine an optimal response to the pandemic, many countries, communities and friendship groups compare their own
group to other groups – most obviously by looking at tables of infection rates,
deaths and testing numbers (e.g., those provided by Johns Hopkins University,
2020). The outcome of that comparison is important, because the sense that one's
group (e.g., one's country or region) is doing poorly or well will dictate, among
other things, whether a group feels it can relax restrictions on social gathering or
else needs to tighten them.

We also compare our ingroups to those outgroups that are seen to provide a
relevant basis for social comparison. Indeed, because many countries did not see
China as a relevant comparison group when the first outbreak of COVID-19 was
reported from Wuhan, they did not take appropriate measures to stop the spread
of the virus. For example, it has been argued that one reason why Italy was slow
to respond to the outbreak was that its citizens did not compare themselves with
China but instead with other European countries. As Italy's Undersecretary of
State for Health, Sandra Zampa, observed:

Most importantly, Italy looked at the example of China, Ms. Zampa said, not as a practical warning, but as a 'science fiction movie that had nothing to do with us.' And when the virus exploded, Europe, she said, 'looked at us the same way we looked at China'. (Horowitz, Bubola, & Povoledo, 2020)

In the context of such comparisons, groups and their leaders wanted to establish a sense of positive social identity by making it clear that they had responded to the outbreak better than other groups. Accordingly, throughout the crisis, many national leaders pointed to ways in which their own country's response was superior to that of others. For instance, at a press briefing on April 2, Australia's Prime Minister, Scott Morrison, boasted that 'we have mobilised a testing regime better than any in the world' (*Rev*, 2020). Similarly, Israel's Prime Minister, Benjamin Netanyahu, tweeted that 'Israel has been ranked first in the COVID-19 Health Safety Countries Ranking on the Deep Knowledge Group website' (Weinglass, 2020). The fact that no other leaders made reference to the work of the Deep Knowledge Group speaks too to the fact that in order to achieve a positive sense of social identity, we are often very selective both in the measures we use to compare ourselves to others and in the groups we compare ourselves with (in ways that social identity theory predicts; Tajfel & Turner, 1979). Thus, on April 27 President Donald Trump claimed that 'the United States has produced dramatically better health outcomes than any other country, with the possible exception of Germany' – but this was true only because he compared the US with a small number of countries that had been hit hard by the first wave of the virus (e.g., Italy, Spain, the UK; Mackey, 2020).

While group members look to make intergroup comparisons that put their ingroup in a positive light, these efforts are also constrained by social reality. In particular, society is highly stratified – with some groups having a lot more status and power than others. Unlike their low-status counterparts, high-status groups by definition already compare favourably on key status-defining dimensions in ways that give them a positive social identity. It is therefore not surprising that the primary interest of advantaged groups is in maintaining and protecting their dominant position. In contrast, lower status groups often struggle to achieve a positive identity because intergroup comparisons typically confirm their inferior status in ways that make the group unattractive and unviable. As we will see in the chapters that follow, group status is an important determinant of responses to COVID-19 – not least because this is something that the virus can threaten. In particular, groups that have a lot to lose (e.g., retail businesses, sporting bodies) can be expected to press vigorously for actions that preserve their status (e.g., ending the lockdown, financial stimulus), while those that have little to lose (e.g., environmental groups) may see the virus as an important opportunity for social change.

Social identities are shaped by history, context and influence

Social comparisons with other groups help us to understand who 'we' are, but which social identities, out of myriad possible ones, do we use to define ourselves in any given context? Andrew may be an academic, an active member of his local community, a Liverpool fan, and Northern Irish, but which group membership will inform his sense of self – and hence his behaviour – in any given context? Indeed, if we assume that all of these social groups embrace different norms about how to respond to COVID-19 (e.g., so that his local community supports physical distancing but his soccer team does not), how do we know which norms Andrew will internalise and comply with?

Broadly speaking, the social identity approach suggests that three sets of factors are at play here (Oakes, Haslam, & Turner, 1994). The first factor is a person's *social history*. This means that Andrew is more likely to define himself in terms of a given social identity if the group membership that this relates to has been important for him and his fellow group members in the past (in self-categorization theory, this is referred to as the principle of *perceiver readiness*). The second factor is *social context* (Haslam & Turner, 1992). This means that the identities we use as a basis for self-definition need to be meaningful in the situation at hand. Andrew is more likely to define himself as a Liverpool fan when he is watching a football match (especially with other Liverpool fans) than when at an academic conference. In the context of COVID-19, he is also more likely to define himself as Irish if he sees the situation he confronts as one which other Irish people are confronting too, and as being different from that faced by members of other groups (e.g., Germans). This is the principle of *fit*. The third factor is *social influence* (Reicher, Haslam, & Hopkins, 2005). This means that the way we define ourselves is also shaped by the ways that others – particularly other ingroup members – encourage us to define ourselves. For example, if other people who Andrew identifies with define themselves as British, rather than Northern Irish (and make this identity seem more fitting), then he is more likely to do so too.

Yet while these three factors interact to determine *which* social identities we use to define ourselves, features of the broader socio-structural context also determine *whether* we define ourselves primarily as group members or as individuals. Tajfel and Turner (1979) argued that people are more likely to define themselves as group members when they see this as the best way to achieve a positive sense of identity. At least three factors have a bearing on this: (1) the perceived status of the group, (2) the perceived permeability of group boundaries (i.e., opportunity to leave the group), and (3) the possibility of changing the group's circumstances. These factors make people less likely to define themselves in terms of a given group membership if that group has low status, if it is possible to leave the group, or if the group's status seems unlikely to change (Ellemers, 1993).

This also means that if a group is unattractive (e.g., because it is stigmatised or disadvantaged) then its members are likely to try to 'go it alone' if they sense that this offers them the best pathway to self-advancement. Indeed, this way of thinking can be seen to underpin — and to have been reinforced by — individualistic ideologies of meritocracy and personal mobility that have come to the fore in recent decades (particularly in Western societies). These were famously embraced by the Conservative British Prime Minister Margaret Thatcher in her observation that:

> There is no such thing as society. There are individual men and women, and there are families. And no government can do anything except through people, and people must look to themselves first. It's our duty to look after ourselves. (Evans, 2004, p. 106)

Such a philosophy encourages people to act in terms of personal rather than social identity — and therefore to turn their back on their groups and the plight of fellow group members. If you are a woman or black and you experience sexism or racism, do not work with others to fight for social justice. Just lean in or walk on by.

As we have already seen, in the face of a pandemic, such a mindset has the potential to be fatal. At the same time (and in many ways rather fortunately), in pandemics and other large-scale disasters, the factors that we have discussed also serve to make people more likely to define themselves in terms of shared social identity (Drury, 2012). In particular, the context is one that makes shared group memberships (e.g., those based on nationality) both more meaningful and more inescapable. Moreover, because leaders recognise the value of social identity as a resource for bringing people together, this is something that they typically seek to cultivate. Thus, it was no accident that, early on in the pandemic, Prime Minister Boris Johnson chose to deliberately push back against his Conservative predecessor's earlier pronouncement by declaring that, indeed, 'there really is such a thing as society' (Braddock, 2020). In the process, he signalled a more inclusive approach to the COVID-19 crisis and opened the door to a broad set of positive social resources which flow from people seeing themselves — and acting — not as isolated individuals but as members of a collective who are 'all in this together'.

Social identity provides a platform for social influence, social connection, collective behaviour and intergroup relations

Having sketched out the processes that lead people to define themselves in terms of a particular group membership, the obvious question is why does this matter – and in particular, why does this help us to understand the psychology of COVID-19? In many ways, this is a question that the rest of this book seeks to answer. In particular, we seek to show how the social identity approach provides the conceptual tools to address each of the key issues that we raised at the end of the previous chapter. In the sections that follow we will therefore show how a sense of group membership (i.e., *self-categorisation* in terms of social identity, or a sense of 'us-ness') is the basis for (a) social influence and effective leadership, (b) social connection and hence health, (c) solidarity and collective behaviour, and (d) long-term social relations between groups. These links are represented schematically in Figure 2.

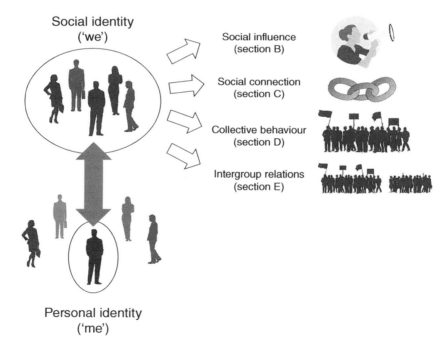

Figure 2 Social identity as a basis for social influence, social connection, collective behaviour and intergroup relations

A first point to note is that social identity is a platform for *social influence* (Turner, 1991). More specifically, as we explain in some detail in Section B, our willingness to listen to, and be guided by, another person (in particular, a leader) is contingent on us (a) defining ourselves in terms of social identity and then (b) believing that that person is representative of it (so that, in the language of categorization theory, they are *prototypical* of the group; Rosch, 1978). In these terms, it is clear that effective leadership during the COVID-19 crisis has centred on leaders being able both to develop a sense of a shared identity (a sense that 'we are in this together') and to be seen as 'one of us' (Haslam, Reicher, & Platow, 2011). This is seen, for example, in the words and actions of Scandinavian Prime Ministers Mette Frederiksen (Denmark), Sanna Marin (Finland) and Erna Solberg (Norway), all of whom went to great efforts both to bind their societies together and to be seen to stand with them (e.g., Tu, 2020). This in turn allowed them to enforce tough physical distancing measures because, for their citizens, compliance did not feel like a personal sacrifice but as the 'right and proper thing to do to protect us'.

As well as being the basis for influence, even more fundamentally, social identity is a basis for *social connection*. Indeed, while early social identity theorising (in the wake of the minimal groups studies) focused on explaining intergroup hostility and discrimination, it is increasingly recognised that the groups we identify with provide us with important psychological resources (Haslam, Jetten et al., 2018; Jetten, Haslam, & Haslam, 2012). In particular, they help us to 'know who we are' in ways that give our lives meaning and purpose, and a sense of self-worth and control. Our ingroups are also an important source of social support in times of stress, as we have seen throughout the COVID-19 crisis. However, in this context, we also see an important corollary of this – namely, that when we are cut off from groups that are important to us (e.g., our extended family, friends, work teams, sports clubs), this can have negative consequences for our health and well-being. While COVID-19 clearly harms people's health directly, so too can the social isolation that results from the measures used to deal with it. These are issues that we work through in Section C. Here we also examine whether defining groups as ingroups or outgroups leads us to see them as a source of either safety and support, or of threat and harm – in ways that have profound implications for health-relevant behaviour.

Will COVID-19 bring us closer together or pull us apart? Speaking to the latter possibility, there has been widespread discussion of the ways in which fears of contamination can bring out the worst in us (e.g., Rathje, 2020). The media has also extensively reported on hoarding and panic buying in ways that sometimes give the impression that during this pandemic, everyone is out for themselves. However, in many ways the bigger picture is a much more positive one.

So, despite the fact that every other human is a potential source of infection (and hence a threat to life), during the pandemic we have witnessed a range of novel and powerful forms of solidarity and *collective behaviour* in communities and society more generally. In ways that we explain in Section D, all of these can be understood as manifestations of an emergent sense of shared social identity. This indeed explains why panic and selfishness are the exception, not the rule.

Yet as we noted in Chapter 1, there is a dark side to COVID-19 too. Not least, this is because the virus has put a magnifying glass on social inequalities. Indeed, it is clear that the suffering brought about by the virus has fallen unfairly on the shoulders of lower status groups in society and the lower status countries. In ways that social identity theory would predict, this is a recipe for social unrest and challenges to the status quo. Some predict that social discontent will flare up as soon as bans are lifted and individuals are free to move again. As Kluth (2020) observes:

> It would be naive to think that, once this medical emergency is over, either individual countries or the world can carry on as before. Anger and bitterness will find new outlets. Early harbingers include millions of Brazilians banging pots and pans from their windows to protest against their government, or Lebanese prisoners rioting in their over-crowded jails.

We put these possibilities under the microscope in Section E. In particular, we explore how COVID-19 is likely to impact *intergroup relations* by changing things that social identity research tells us are important: the permeability of group boundaries, the legitimacy of intergroup relations, and the nature of the social identities which we define ourselves (Tajfel & Turner, 1979). These shifts, we suggest, will help us understand the long-term impact of COVID-19 – not only on the forces at play in society, but also on its very structure.

SECTION
B SOCIAL INFLUENCE

Efforts to influence people loom large in a pandemic. In particular, there is a demand for effective leadership that explains what is going on and motivates people to contribute to the achievement of shared group goals. There are two key reasons why this has been critical for the management of COVID-19. The first is that the virus has created a pressing need for people to work together to achieve new collective goals. Medical staff need to attend to the unwell, workers in a range of sectors need to maintain stretched services, and the general public need to do what they can to minimise the burden on those services and to halt the spread of the virus. The second reason is that there is considerable uncertainty about the nature of the virus and how to respond to it. People therefore look to others – and to leaders in particular – to help them understand what they should be thinking and doing, as well as how their actions contribute to a concerted societal response. As well as wanting coherent and convincing explanations of these things, people also want leaders who *inspire* them and others to put their shoulders to the collective wheel, in order to 'do whatever it takes' to endure the crisis and come out in the best possible shape on the other side.

In this section we look at multiple facets of the influence process that have been foregrounded during the COVID-19 pandemic, starting with an examination of the psychology of effective *leadership* (Chapter 3). This is followed by an analysis of the dynamics of *followership and compliance* (Chapter 4), *behaviour change* (Chapter 5) and the spread of *conspiracy theories* (Chapter 6). The key message here is that all of these influence processes are grounded in a sense of shared social identity ('us-ness') within a given community. Accordingly, in order to secure compliance and desired forms of influence, the first priority of would-be influencers (e.g., leaders) is to cultivate this feeling of 'us-ness'. In short, they need to be entrepreneurs of identity who make sure there is an 'us' to rally behind.

3

Leadership

S. Alexander Haslam

Since COVID-19 first began spreading around the world, there have been myriad examples of leadership that has not only motivated people to work for collective goals, but has also helped them understand how best they can do this. Two examples are Jürgen Klopp's address to Liverpool fans early on in the crisis on March 13, and Queen Elizabeth II's televised address to the British public and members of the Commonwealth on April 6. Klopp had the challenging task of letting fans know that their bid for a first Premiership in 30 years had been halted by COVID-19, but did so by pointing out that 'if it's a choice between football and the good of the wider society, it's no contest' (Klopp, 2020). 'First and foremost', he observed, 'all of us have to do whatever we can to protect one another. In society I mean. This should be the case all the time in life, but in this moment, I think it matters more than ever.' Likewise, the Queen zeroed in on the need for solidarity and collective steadfastness in her address:

> Together we are tackling this disease, and I want to reassure you that if we remain united and resolute, then we will overcome it. I hope in the years to come everyone will be able to take pride in how they responded to this challenge. And those who come after us will say the Britons of this generation were as strong as any. That the attributes of self-discipline, of quiet good-humoured resolve and of fellow-feeling still characterise this country. The pride in who we are is not a part of our past, it defines our present and our future. (Stubley, 2020)

Nevertheless, in the first months of the COVID-19 crisis there were a great many occasions on which leaders' efforts at influence and mobilisation fell short. We will not dwell on these here, but in this chapter we want to ask what precisely it is that makes leaders more or less successful in their attempts to recruit the energies of others to their cause. What is it, for example, that led people (including Liverpool's rivals and committed non-royalists) not just to applaud Klopp's and the Queen's leadership, but to engage in acts of *followership* that translated their calls for mutual care and compassion into action? This, indeed, is *the* critical question – for the ultimate proof of leadership is not how impressive a leader looks or sounds, but what they lead others to *do* in the name of the group they lead (Bennis, 1999; Platow, Haslam, Reicher, & Steffens, 2015).

As we foreshadowed in the opening section of this book, our answer to this question centres on the dynamics of social identity. More specifically, we argue that leaders' capacity to motivate others is grounded in what we refer to as their *identity leadership* (Steffens et al., 2014) – their ability to represent and advance the shared interests of group members and to create and embed a sense of *shared social identity* among them (a sense of 'us-ness'; see Haslam et al., 2011). For leaders, then, this sense of us-ness is the key resource that they need to marshal in order to secure the support and toil of others. Accordingly, we see that this sense of shared social identity was pivotal to the communications of both Klopp and the Queen, with Klopp using the terms 'we', 'us' and 'our' 17 times in a text of 381 words and the Queen referring to these collective pronouns 27 times in a speech of 524 words (i.e., once every 22 words and once every 19 words respectively). Indeed, the power of such language is confirmed in previous research which found that politicians who win elections use collective pronouns once every 79 words, while those who lose elections use them only once every 136 words (Steffens & Haslam, 2013).

We can enlarge upon this analysis by outlining three key ways in which leaders need to manage social identity in order to be effective: (a) by *representing us*, (b) by *doing it for us*, and (c) by *crafting and embedding a sense of us*. These things have previously been shown to underpin effective leadership in a broad range of contexts – most notably, in a global study of effective organisational leadership conducted in 22 different countries and covering all six inhabited continents (van Dick et al., 2018). They have also very much come to the fore in mobilising responses to COVID-19.

Leaders need to represent us, and in a crisis 'us' becomes more inclusive

As noted above, one way that people have dealt with the uncertainty and fear created by COVID-19 is by turning to leaders for information and reassurance.

But in a world where much is unproven and unknown, who do we perceive to be in a position to provide this? The answer is those with whom we share social identity and who are *prototypical members of our ingroups*, who best represent our values, our interests, and our perspective on the world (Haslam, 2001; Hogg, 2001; Turner & Haslam, 2001). This in turn means that those who are prototypical of 'us' are in the best position to exert influence (i.e., leadership) over us.

The significance of this point has been apparent since the start of the COVID-19 crisis, where it is clear that people's responses to news of the virus were shaped by opinion leaders who reflected their political preferences. In particular, leading conservative platforms in Western countries (e.g., *Fox News* in the US, *Sky News* in Australia) argued that the virus was a hysterical left-wing hoax, and that there was no need for alarm (Gabbatt, 2020; Jones, 2020). As a result, it was apparent that in the early weeks of COVID-19's spread through many Western countries, conservatives were much less likely than liberals to take health warnings seriously and to make adjustments to their daily lives (Heath, 2020; see also Chapter 17).

However, as the scale of the problem posed by the virus increased, it became clear that there was a requirement for national leaders to represent shared national identities rather than their narrower political allegiances. Accordingly, most leaders showed a marked increase in the inclusivity of their rhetoric (although there were notable exceptions; e.g., in Brazil, India, and the US). As the Australian Prime Minister, Scott Morrison, put it, 'There are no blue teams or red teams. There are no more unions or bosses. There are just Australians now' (C. Johnson, 2020). At the same time too, leaders' status as prototypical representatives of a national 'us' was consolidated because a rising spirit of national unity made it harder for those leaders' opponents either to criticise them or to gain the limelight themselves (Stewart, 2020).

One important upshot of this embrace of inclusive national (vs. exclusive party political) identities was a sharp uplift in leaders' popularity, a pattern seen previously in the wake of other national disasters (e.g., 9/11; Schubert, Stewart, & Curran, 2002). Whereas previously leaders' support had come largely from their own political base, now their appeal extended beyond party lines. Indeed, in March 2020 the approval levels of leaders of 10 of the world's biggest democracies rose by an average of 9%, with most of that rise attributable to an increase in support from non-aligned voters (Stacey & Pickard, 2020). Moreover, it appears that the extent of this rise was itself a reflection of leaders' ability to embody the collective spirit of their nations – something that was appreciably more marked in countries like the UK, Canada and New Zealand than it was in places like the US, Japan and Brazil (Leaders League, 2020).

Leaders need to be seen to do it for us, and there is no place for leader exceptionalism

In a time of crisis, people want not only leaders who represent them and their shared concerns, but also leaders who *do things* to address those concerns. In particular, people look to leaders to take the initiative and develop policies that respond in meaningful ways to the crisis they collectively confront. To the extent that such actions are seen to be motivated by broad concern for the community, support for them often comes from unlikely quarters. In Australia, for example, the Conservative Morrison government recruited former union leader Greg Combet to help develop its business strategy and manage employee relations – something neither party would have deemed conscionable prior to the crisis (McCulloch, 2020).

A corollary of this is that if leaders are seen to be looking after their own personal interests (i.e., 'doing it for me'), they will be a target of opprobrium. For this reason, there was widespread condemnation of US Senators Burr, Loeffler, Inhofe, and Feinstein when reports emerged that they had sold off shares after gaining privileged access to information about the likely impact of COVID-19 on the US stockmarket (Zabollis-Roig, 2020). Indeed, where leaders appear to hold themselves above the group and its standards, this will often be the kiss of death. Thus, Scotland's Chief Medical Officer, Catherine Calderwood, was made to walk the plank after flouting her own Department's advice to reduce unnecessary travel (Carrell, 2020), as was the New Zealand Health Minister, David Clark, after violating his own government's lockdown by going mountain biking (McKay, 2020).

So while leaders may be tempted to see themselves as exceptions to group rules, any such decoupling can be fatal for public trust. Moreover, the key problem with leader exceptionalism of this form is that by seeming to place the leader above the group it undermines the sense of shared identity that leaders depend on in order to lead successfully. As the Scottish Labour leader, Richard Leonard, said of Calderwood's lapse, it is 'running the serious risk of causing public confidence to collapse. This is in no-one's interest at a time of national crisis' (Carrell, 2020).

Leaders need to craft and embed a sense of us, and this creates a platform for citizenship

A final point about the link between leadership and social identity is that both require hard work. Leadership proves appreciably easier if leaders have prepared for a crisis by developing a response capacity and appropriate contingency plans (Jetten, Fielding, Crimston, Mols, & Haslam, 2020). As we and others have previously observed, responses to natural disasters such as floods and earthquakes are also far more effective when the people they affect have a pre-existing sense of shared social identity (Muldoon et al., 2019; Williams & Drury, 2009). Nevertheless, this sense of shared identity is never something that leaders can take for granted, and it always has to be worked on. More particularly, they need to be *identity entrepreneurs* and *identity impresarios* who strive to build and then embed a shared sense of 'us' within the groups they lead (Haslam et al., 2011).

Clear examples of this were provided in the early COVID-related communications of the New Zealand Prime Minister, Jacinda Ardern. In contrast to similar messages in other countries (see Figure 3), these went to great pains to explain not

Alex Haslam
@alexanderhaslam

Australia and New Zealand's original COVID-19 alerts side-by-side. These two messages exemplify the difference between old-fashioned leadership ("just give them the information") and identity leadership ("let's work on this together").

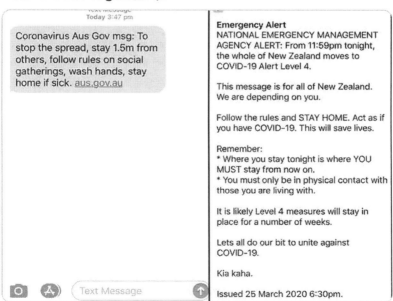

Figure 3   The importance of identity leadership

just what New Zealanders needed to do, but why this was essential for the country as a whole. As she put it:

> The Government will do all it can to protect you. Now I'm asking you to do everything you can to protect us all. None of us can do this alone. Your actions will be critical to our collective ability to stop the spread of COVID-19. Failure to play your part in the coming days will put the lives of others at risk. There will be no tolerance for that and we will not hesitate in using enforcement powers if needed. We're in this together and must unite against COVID-19. (TVNZ, 2020)

Such efforts of identity leadership are critical because the shared social identity that leaders cultivate provides the all-important psychological platform for the coordination of collective efforts to tackle the challenges that the group as a whole faces (Haslam & Reicher, 2006). Indeed, without this platform of shared social identity, there is a risk that people will eschew acts of citizenship in which they look out for each other (e.g., by engaging in physical distancing or adhering to quarantine), and instead embrace a philosophy of 'everyone for themselves' (see also Chapter 18). Effective identity leadership thus serves the dual function of (a) holding groups together through a crisis and (b) constructively channelling the energies of group members in ways that increase the likelihood of positive outcomes.

The importance of identity leadership for the management of COVID-19 was highlighted by the Canadian Broadcasting Company's Justin McElroy when he reflected on the success of British Columbia in containing the spread of the virus. This, he argued, had much to do with the hard work the province's Chief Medical Health Officer, Dr Bonnie Henry, had done to build an open and inclusive relationship of mutual trust with her fellow British Columbians:

> Given that part of this response depends on being altruistic and doing the right thing to help other people who we will never meet, having a leader who can articulate how we're all in this together and make a convincing case for why you need to do your part … is very important. (McElroy, 2020)

In short, the key to successful leadership is not simply to talk about everybody being 'in this together', but to do everything in one's power to ensure that this is their lived experience – and that you are representative of it.

4

Compliance and Followership

Niklas K. Steffens

COVID-19 has posed a significant challenge, with whole nations striving to coordinate their activities in response to the pandemic. In the process, it has been critical for people to follow advice and comply with policies in an effort to solve problems through effective forms of coordination and cooperation. In this chapter, we define *compliance* as a person's acquiescence with a request (Cialdini & Goldstein, 2004). The related, broader concept of *followership* (or following behaviour) refers to individuals' actions in responding to leaders or to those in authority (Uhl-Bien , Riggio, Lowe, & Carsten, 2014). Here we explore a number of big questions about these processes. What drives compliance and followership? When do people choose *not* to comply with advice or regulations? What are helpful (and not so helpful) forms of followership?

In the context of the COVID-19 response, our answers focus on three key factors that drive compliance and followership: (a) the internalisation of *collective* concerns, (2) the behaviour of *other members* of people's groups and communities, and (3) *trust* in government and its leaders.

Acts of followership are not individual in nature but result from the internalisation of collective concerns

There are a range of traditional ways of thinking about why people follow the instructions of others. One of the most influential of these argues that people have a strong and inherent tendency to 'blindly' follow the orders of leaders, particularly when those leaders are in positions of power. This analysis, which was famously set out by Stanley Milgram (1974) following his research into 'Obedience to Authority', suggests that people don't think too much about *why* they are following, but do so mindlessly and instinctively. Another influential model suggests that followership is a matter of being 'cut out' for particular follower roles, such that some people are engaged followers but others are merely sheep (e.g., Kelley, 1988).

A problem with both these models, however, is that they fail to explain the importance of social context, and, in particular, the importance of the *relationship* between followers and leaders. If followership is a matter of being a particular type of person or of blindly following orders, why does one find the same person following some instructions vigilantly and ignoring others?

Looking at the evidence, we discover that contrary to Milgram's claims, ordering people to do something generally fosters *dis*obedience rather than obedience (Haslam, Reicher, & Birney, 2014). Indeed, unless people (a) see themselves as part of a larger collective 'we' (e.g., as 'us New Yorkers') and (b) identify with the cause of that collective, then they are unlikely to compromise on their personal self-interest (Haslam & Reicher, 2017). Accordingly, rather than ordering people to engage in particular behaviours (e.g., refraining from stockpiling scarce resources), it is generally more effective to request that they do so as part of an *appeal* to group-based sensibilities.

These observations are backed by evidence which suggests that people want to be respected and treated fairly *in terms of a group membership that they share* with policy makers (e.g., as Canadians, as Scots), and that if they feel that they are disrespected or treated unfairly, they are unlikely to fall in line (Tyler & Blader, 2003). Consistent with this, social identification with the authority or institution that applies a policy has been shown to underpin compliance with that policy (Bradford, Hohl, Jackson, & MacQueen, 2015). Similar patterns have also been found for compliance with tax law (Hartner, Kirchler, Poschalko, & Rechberger, 2010) and adherence to mandatory and discretionary rules set out by one's employer (Blader & Tyler, 2009).

Compliance is shaped by perceptions of the behaviour of other members of our communities

People's willingness to comply is also shaped by *norms*. These derive from our understandings of what other people – particularly those in the groups we identify with – think and do (Smith & Louis, 2008). Accordingly, communications about social norms can be used to influence and mobilise others (for good or bad;

Cialdini et al., 2006; Fehr & Fischbacher, 2004; see Chapter 17). Indeed, there is evidence that perceptions of norms influence a range of citizenship behaviours, including littering (Cialdini, Reno, & Kallgren, 1990), recycling (Abbott, Nandeibam, & O'Shea, 2013), cooperation (Thøgersen, 2008) and compliance with tax law (Wenzel, 2004).

As the COVID-19 pandemic has unfolded, people's cooperation with directives has been affected by the degree to which the behaviour in question was seen as both acceptable and widespread. By extension, this suggests that news reports that single out infrequent non-compliant behaviours can be problematic, because they suggest that non-compliant behaviour is prevalent and normative. For example, images of people apparently failing to practise physical distancing or engaging in 'panic buying' can lead people to engage in these practices because they think that doing so is normative (see Figure 4). Ultimately, then, in order to foster compliance and followership it is useful for leaders to bolster their appeals to citizens by referring to other group members and invoking social norms, and, when they do, to craft these appeals in ways that foster cooperative forms of citizenship.

Trust in authorities can facilitate both healthy and fatal forms of followership

When the path ahead is complex and highly uncertain, a core ingredient of people's willingness to follow leaders is their faith in those leaders and their actions. Accordingly, evidence indicates that *trust in leaders and authorities* is critical for leaders' capacity to secure compliance with their policies (Jimenez & Iyer, 2016) and for encouraging followership more generally (Dirks & Skarlicki, 2004). But where does this trust come from?

The first thing to note is that the trust we have in leaders is not something that is fixed and immutable. Rather, like credit in the bank, it is something that is gained (or lost) over time as a function of leaders' perceived contribution and service (or lack thereof) to the group they lead. More specifically, we trust a given leader to the extent that we consistently see him or her as 'one of us' who is 'doing it for us' (Giessner & van Knippenberg, 2008; Platow et al., 2015).

But when people see their leaders as being 'one of us', this comes with some level of risk because it licenses leaders to take the group into uncharted terrain (Abrams, Randsley de Moura, & Travaglino, 2013). In the case of COVID-19, this licence has been used to encourage both health-promoting and health-debilitating forms of followership. For example, trust in President Trump's suggestion that one might use malaria drugs (or even household disinfectants;

Ullrich Ecker
@UlliEcker

Good to be aware of how "wrong" photos are used to mislead people about the social norms of social distancing 👇

🔵 **Luke W** @alukeonlife · Apr 27

Ok... buckle up, have I got a thread for you on rage inducing photos!

Our story begins earlier today and this "shocking" photo of people allegedly not social distancing at Bournemouth beach

Show this thread

8:28 AM · Apr 29, 2020 · Twitter for Android

Figure 4 Evidence of other people apparently failing to comply encourages non-compliance

Rogers, Hauser, Yuhas, & Haberman, 2020) to combat COVID-19 proved fatal for some of those who followed his advice (Waldrop, 2020).

On the other side of the ledger (and the planet), New Zealand's Prime Minister, Jacinda Ardern, delivered personable messages from her living room that showed her to be very much a 'regular' New Zealander (Roy, 2020b) and thereby helped secure a high level of compliance with an extreme lockdown. Moreover, her message highlighted that the sacrifice she was asking New Zealanders to make was not for her, nor for themselves as individuals, but for the nation as a whole:

I have one final message. Be kind. I know people will want to act as enforcers. And I understand that, people are afraid and anxious. We will play that role for you. What we need from you, is support one another. Go home tonight and check in on your neighbours. Start a phone tree with your street. Plan how you'll keep in touch with one another. We will get through this together, but only if we stick together. (Ardern, 2020)

In this message, Ardern distils the essence of a social identity perspective on followership: recognising that this is grounded in the strength of group-based ties between the leader and their group. Accordingly, her message focuses followers' attention not on herself, but on the group and her commitment to it. This then encourages followers to do the same.

5

Behaviour Change

Frank Mols

On March 11 2020, the World Health Organization (WHO) issued a statement confirming that COVID-19 was a pandemic. WHO experts advised that from this point onwards, governments' main challenge would be to 'bend the curve downwards' as this would help to prevent a surge in infections and stop hospital Intensive Care Units (ICUs) becoming overwhelmed. What added weight to the WHO's calls were examples of countries that had already lost control of the virus, and were now facing large numbers of fatalities due to ICUs being overrun (e.g., Italy, Spain). Eager to avoid repeating this scenario, most other governments acted swiftly, urging their citizens to wash their hands more often, to keep their distance from each other, and to avoid crowds. Some countries went further and introduced forced lockdowns (e.g., France, New Zealand). Nevertheless, other countries (e.g., the UK, Netherlands, Sweden) initially deviated from WHO advice by pursuing an approach that sought to expose people to the novel coronavirus and thereby develop 'herd immunity' to it.

This chapter critiques the model of human frailty on which this decision was based (a model that we first discussed in Chapter 1). As a counterpoint to this, it suggests that social identity processes are a key source of human strength, and that leaders who tap into these are best positioned to drive the forms of behaviour change required in order to defeat COVID-19.

Government policy to address COVID-19 was initially dictated by concerns about human weakness

In the case of the UK, there are several possible reasons why its leadership was initially reluctant to enact recommended physical distancing measures. First, the government was concerned that physical distancing measures would have to be sustained for a long period of time, placing a heavy burden on the UK economy and risking compliance 'fatigue' (Hahn, Chater, Lagnado, & Osman, 2020; Mills, 2020). A second, related reason was that successive Conservative governments had become enthralled with behavioural economics – a trend started by David Cameron's government, which established the UK Behavioural Insights Team (BIT) in 2010. Several sources have suggested that it was BIT chief executive David Halpern who first floated the idea of going down the path of 'herd-immunity' (Boseley, 2020), and who first warned that citizens could fall victim to physical distancing 'fatigue' (Sodha, 2020). This, however, is something he has consistently denied (Conn et al., 2020). Yet regardless of its precise source, an unintended consequence of this commitment to behavioural economics was that, in line with the core logic of this framework, key policy makers had come to see ordinary citizens as error-prone and weak.

It seems likely that these twin factors explain why, when seeking to manage the COVID-19 crisis, the UK government relied for so long on relatively minimal behavioural interventions (e.g., amusing adverts to encourage people to wash their hands and keep their distance from each other), and why it took so long to embrace lockdown strategies. This was the thrust of an open letter signed by 681 social scientists expressing concern about the lack of evidence to support the idea that a weak public would quickly become tired of complying with government directives (Mills, 2020).

More generally, as several commentators noted, the UK government's initial policy settings reflected a bleak view of its citizens' psychology and willpower, seeing them as having limited capacity 'to do the right thing' and thereby making herd-contamination inevitable (Yates, 2020). Similar criticisms emerged in the Netherlands, where the government's commitment to behavioural economics had led it to underestimate citizens' capacity to sustain physical distancing (Dujardin, 2020).

Governments increasingly seek to change social behaviour via 'nudges'

> They're [the] rules that need to be in place, and everybody must follow them and stay at home wherever possible. . . . we've set those rules, we're enforcing against those rules, and we reiterate those rules, because that is the best way to be able to bend the curve down and stop the spread of the virus. (Hancock, 2020)

As this statement from the British Health Secretary, Matt Hancock, illustrates, governments facing crises often resort to the default strategy of seeking to secure policy compliance through top-down legislation and enforcement. However, in recent decades they have increasingly experimented with new 'modes of governance'. One such mode is *liberal* (or *soft*) *paternalism* (Thaler & Sunstein, 2003). This is informed by a belief that citizens should retain choice over their actions but nevertheless be given 'steers' – notably in the form of subtle behavioural '*nudges*' – to encourage them to behave in particular ways that are 'good' for them and society. In this vein, governments around the Western world have resorted to a range of tried-and-tested nudges to encourage citizens to do such things as recycle, save for retirement, and sign up for organ donation. Evidence suggests that this approach can be quite effective when dealing with relatively uncomplicated policy issues (e.g., as documented in Thaler & Sunstein, 2009). However, this effectiveness is less proven when it comes to dealing with complex (a.k.a. 'wicked') policy issues.

Liberal paternalism (and behavioural economics more generally) is underpinned by a notion that humans are imperfect information processors whose capacity to make sound decisions is compromised by a propensity to resort to cognitive shortcuts. This model has a long pedigree in social psychology (and social science more generally). It flows directly from the view that humans are 'cognitive misers' who generally process and respond to social information in a way that minimises intellectual demands but introduces error (after Fiske & Taylor, 1984; for critiques see Gigerenzer, 2018; Oakes et al., 1994).

The core idea here is that there is too much information in the world for people to process it all. Instead, people 'make do' by relying on heuristics (i.e., cognitive rules of thumb) that provide an understanding that is generally 'good enough' for their purposes but nevertheless susceptible to error and bias. One example of such a heuristic is the *availability bias* – the tendency to attend and give more weight to information that is readily accessible than information that is not (Tversky & Kahneman, 1973). The logic behind nudges is that such biases can be reverse-engineered and exploited in ways that make particular 'good' behaviours more likely. For example, policy makers might make use of the availability bias by providing people with a list of behavioural options where those behaviours that they want people to engage in are prominent, while those they seek to discourage are less prominent or absent.

The idea that people can be nudged covertly in this way is not new. As Robert Cialdini (1984) showed in his book *Influence*, marketing experts have perennially resorted to various covert behaviour change techniques to increase sales. However, the idea that governments might encourage particular behaviours by changing the 'choice architecture' that surrounds them was popularised more recently through best-selling books like *Nudge* (Thaler & Sunstein, 2009) and *Thinking, Fast and Slow* (Kahneman, 2011). Although sceptics continue to question whether nudging is ethical (Engelen & Schmidt, 2020) and best regarded as a passing fad (McDaid & Merkur, 2014), this has done nothing to hold back the rapid proliferation of Behavioural Insights Teams (or 'nudge units') advising governments around the world on how to best shape their citizens' behaviour.

Radical behaviour change requires identity-based norm internalisation

There is growing consensus that, on their own, nudges have limited usefulness as tools for achieving radical forms of large-scale behaviour change. As we have argued elsewhere, the main problem here is that nudges fail to secure *norm internalisation* (Mols, Haslam, Jetten, & Steffens, 2015). While it is possible to use nudges to change behaviours that are passive and produce unthinking compliance, nudges are ineffective in securing behaviour changes that require deep commitment to a new course of collective action organised around a common cause. Of course, COVID-19 has required just such a course of action.

Without norm internalisation, 'old habits' would be expected to reappear as soon as the choice architecture is reversed. For example, while customers can be nudged into staying at least 1.5 metres away from one another by using floor marking, or into cleaning their hands by placing a hand sanitiser next to a door, once the floor marking or hand sanitiser are no longer present, people return to their former unsafe ways. Moreover, unless relevant norms are in place, they still may never 'do the right thing'. So, while such interventions would go some way to reduce the short-term spread of the virus, what is required to secure *lasting* behaviour change (and avoid gradual fatigue) is a deep commitment to new ways of behaving, underpinned by a sense that this is the right thing for 'us' to do.

The main way to achieve behaviour change of this form is through overt appeals to people's memberships in valued groups – that is, those who define their group-based sense of self. Only when people have come to define themselves in terms of a given group membership (e.g., as German) and believe that certain forms of behaviour are normative for that group – and indeed *required* in order to secure its future – will they be motivated to do the hard work that is needed for behaviour change. Moreover, as this belief is identity-enhancing, it is inherently rewarding and it will seem less like hard work (Cruwys, Norwood, Chachay, Ntontis, & Sheffield, 2020). In contrast to the logic of nudge, this leadership casts and treats citizens not as sheep, but as lions whose strength emerges when they work in tandem to achieve shared goals (Steffens, Haslam, Jetten, & Mols, 2018).

Looking outside the UK, it is clear that many leaders' first instinct was to adopt precisely this model, engaging with citizens as active intelligent agents, rather than as passive cognitive misers, through appeals to shared social identity. For example, it was seen in addresses by Canada's Prime Minister Justin Trudeau (Wherry, 2020) and Germany's Chancellor Angela Merkel (Davidson, 2020). Furthermore, once it became clear that urgent action was needed in order to stop the spread of the COVID-19 virus, the British Prime Minister Boris Johnson himself began to engage in identity entrepreneurship as a central part of his efforts to persuade citizens to follow government advice. In particular, this sense of 'our' collective potential was foregrounded in his address to the nation on March 23:

> Each and every one of us is now obliged to join together, to halt the spread of this disease, to protect our NHS, and to save many, many thousands of lives. . . . And I know that as they have in the past so many times, the people of this country will rise to that challenge. And we will come through it stronger than ever. We will beat the coronavirus and we will beat it together. (Johnson, 2020).

Following this, the UK achieved a rapid 'flattening of the curve' that exceeded the expectations of even the most optimistic epidemiologists (Woodcock, 2020). Tragically, though, the damage of the earlier 'herd-immunity' philosophy had been done, and it was too late to stop Britain recording the highest number of COVID-19 infections and deaths in Europe (Conn et al., 2020).

As outlined in Section A of this book, these two competing models of human psychology, namely behavioural economics and social identity theory (Reicher, Drury, & Stott, 2020b), are of particular relevance to the COVID-19 crisis. The former focuses on individuals *as individuals* and views them pessimistically as 'fragile rationalists' who are prone to error (Reicher, 2020). The latter recognises people's capacity to act and behave *as group members* and offers a more optimistic model of people as collective meaning-makers who – if provided with the right leadership – are capable of exerting themselves for the greater good. The initial phases of responses to the COVID-19 crisis served to bring the differences between these approaches into stark relief, and to expose the inadequacies of a model framed around human deficiency. Certainly, when one is looking for people to behave like lions, it is unhelpful to have only ever thought them capable of behaving like sheep.

6

Conspiracy Theories

Matthew J. Hornsey

It is to get rid of non-productive Chinese in the Chinese community, who are non-productive and in the words of George Bernard Shaw should be eliminated so they don't have to be fed. Secondly, it is either to export the virus into the United States or other parts of the world, or at least fear of the virus. Thirdly, to test whether or not it is possible, through this sort of action, to send the Western world into recession.

(Former Liberal Senator Bronwyn Bishop speaking on *Sky News*; see Baker, 2020)

'Conspiracies' occur when groups of people coordinate secretly to do something unlawful or inappropriate. The difference between a 'conspiracy' and a 'conspiracy theory' is a matter of academic debate, in large part because these things are subjective. People have different standards of proof for deciding whether a conspiracy is real. So one person's conspiracy is another person's conspiracy theory. Given this, the emerging norm is to use the term 'conspiracy' to refer to actual, substantiated events, and to reserve the term 'conspiracy theory' for beliefs that seem, at face value, to be unreasonable or highly speculative (Uscinski, Douglas, & Lewandowsky, 2017). Given the number of converging, credible and independent reports to this effect, it seems reasonable to argue that there was a *conspiracy* within levels of Chinese government to cover up emerging medical advice of a strange new virus that was causing deaths in Wuhan in late 2019. But it would be a *conspiracy theory* to argue, like Bronwyn Bishop, that COVID-19 was part of a Chinese government plan to reduce the state's burden of care by culling vulnerable people.

Sometimes, individual conspiracy theories form part of a more general worldview: that it is commonplace for powerful groups with malevolent intentions to conduct elaborate hoaxes on the public, and to do so in near-perfect secrecy (Goertzel, 2010). This *conspiracist worldview* has also sometimes been called conspiracist ideation or the conspiracy mindset. This worldview makes people open to any non-official account of reality, even when such accounts are inconsistent with each other. For example, survey research shows that the more people believe Princess Diana is still alive, the more they also believe that she was murdered (Wood, Douglas, & Sutton, 2012). Accordingly, it would not be surprising if people were open to inconsistent conspiracy beliefs about COVID-19: for example, that it was invented by China as a biological weapon *and* that it is was developed by Western governments to excuse the introduction of martial law.

Importantly, though, conspiracy theories emerge neither spontaneously nor in a vacuum. More particularly, as we see in the case of Bronwyn Bishop, they are often peddled by leaders and people in positions of authority with a view to shoring up support for a worldview which they represent and are seeking to advance. It is this point that ties this topic both to the concerns of this section and to the work of social identity theorists.

Lack of social identification underpins conspiracist worldviews

The term 'conspiracy theorist' is typically used in a pejorative way, and has become shorthand for people who are prone to woolly thinking and logical fallacies. It is true that conspiracy theorists tend to have relatively low levels of formal education (van Prooijen, 2017), and are prone to intuitive (rather than analytic) thinking (Swami, Voracek, Stieger, Tran, & Furnham, 2014). More than other people, conspiracy theorists tend to see patterns and agency in random events (Douglas, Sutton, Callan, Dawtry, & Harvey, 2016) and show signs of a personality type known as *schizotypy*, characterised by unconventional beliefs, paranoia, and disordered thinking (March & Springer, 2019).

However, focusing on these individual-level factors serves to obscure a more important pattern that emerges in the literature – namely, that conspiracy theorists feel *vulnerable*. Relative to other people, they have low levels of trust in the community and in institutions (Goertzel, 1994). They feel powerless (van Prooijen, 2017) and report feeling low levels of socio-political control (Bruder, Haffke, Neave, Nouripanah, & Imhoff, 2013). In large part, this reflects the fact that people who endorse conspiracy theories – like those who are paranoid more generally (Greenaway, Haslam, & Bingley, 2019) – tend to have low levels of identification with society and its institutions. In other words, they tend to be 'outsiders' and cast themselves as such.

Related to this outsider status, conspiracy theorists are more likely to believe that positive societal norms and values are disintegrating. They have an abstract belief that the world is a dangerous place (Moulding et al., 2016). From this perspective, the emergence of a conspiracist worldview does not stem from poor mental health or illogical thinking (although these may also be present), but rather is a by-product of a lack of identification that engenders feelings of alienation, mistrust, and social disconnection (see Haslam, Jetten et al., 2018). For people who live in authoritarian regimes, the conspiracist worldview can also emerge in response to a history of propaganda, misinformation, and distortion of history from governments and other institutions. Indeed, where official versions of information are unreliable, conspiracist thinking can be a form of rational scepticism or sense-making (van Prooijen, 2019).

To explore these issues in relation to COVID-19, in early March 2020 we collected data from 1,700 people in Australia, the US, and the UK in order to gain insight into the psychology of those who mistrust the official government advice on COVID-19. We gave respondents this prompt:

> For some political and social events it is suggested that the 'official version' of events could be an attempt to hide the truth from the public. . . . When it comes to COVID, what do you think? Please indicate how much you agree or disagree with the following statement: I think that the official version relating to COVID given by the authorities very often hides the truth.

Nearly half of respondents indicated that they 'somewhat agreed', 'agreed', or 'strongly agreed' with this statement. As suggested above, people who agreed were less educated than those who did not, but this effect was weak. More significant was the fact that those who embraced conspiracy theories were more likely than other respondents to feel distressed, lonely, and out of control. In line with previous evidence that paranoia is highest in marginalised members of a community (van Prooijen, Staman, & Krouwel, 2018), conspiracy theories were particularly prevalent among racial minorities (e.g., Asian-Australians, African-Americans). Those who agreed with this statement also had higher estimates of the eventual death rate of COVID-19, suggesting that mistrust of government in this case manifested itself in a sense that the threat posed by COVID-19 was being downplayed.

Conspiracy theories have a social identity dimension

By definition, a conspiracy theory involves beliefs about the actions and agendas of *coalitions* of individuals. Thus, it is difficult to think of a conspiracy that does not have an *intergroup* element, one that crosses ideological, national, ethnic, religious, or political fault lines. For example, an 'us–them' dimension, in which China is understood as an enemy of the West, was clearly a backdrop to Bronwyn Bishop's conspiracy theorising. It is neither a surprise nor a coincidence, then, that Chinese people are more likely to believe that America invented COVID-19, and that Americans are more likely to believe the Chinese government invented it (Chik & Lew, 2020). Indeed, some scholars argue that the predisposition to believe conspiracy theories evolved as an adaptive tendency to be alert to – and to protect against – hostile outgroups (van Prooijen & van Vugt, 2018).

As social identity theorising would also suggest, there is emerging evidence that conspiracy theories can be triggered by intergroup threats and feelings of intergroup powerlessness. For example, anti-Western conspiracy theories in Indonesia are correlated with perceptions of threat (Mashuri, Zaduqisti, Sukmawati, Sakdiah, & Suharini, 2016) and anti-Semitic conspiracy theories in Poland are associated with victimhood-based social identities (Bilewicz, Winiewski, Kofta, & Wójcik, 2013). Furthermore, experimentally induced threats to the status quo in British society (Jolley, Douglas, & Sutton, 2018) and to Muslim identity in Indonesia (Mashuri & Zaduqisti, 2015) led to increased endorsement of conspiracy theories. Conspiracy theories can also be used in a strategic and mindful way, as part of a broader war of disinformation designed to undermine political opponents, deflect scrutiny, promote racism, or recruit terrorists (e.g., Douglas & Sutton, 2018; Jolley, Meleady, & Douglas, 2020; see also Chapter 19).

COVID-19 has all the hallmarks of an event that is ripe for the development of conspiracy theories: it is frightening, it is hard to understand, the causes are complex, and it has resulted in government curtailment of individual freedoms. In such contexts, a lack of identification with official sources of information makes their messages harder to process and to believe (Greenaway, Wright, Willingham, Reynolds, & Haslam, 2015). And as a corollary, those who do not identify with those official sources are much more likely to embrace non-official accounts of reality to help allay their anxiety and regain a sense of control.

Conspiracies about COVID-19 can be grouped together into three broad categories, all of which have a social identity dimension. The first of these argues that the virus was *invented by a powerful outgroup* to advance a malevolent agenda. As noted above, in the case of COVID-19, this is typically claimed to be the American or Chinese governments. Also included in this category are variants of the myth that COVID-19 is caused by 5G technology, as part of a hidden agenda to (for example) reduce the population, force mass vaccination on the public, or facilitate a new world order.

The second category of conspiracy theory argues that the crisis is being *exaggerated in the interests of a powerful outgroup*. In this vein, conspiracy theorists claimed that the threat posed by the virus was being deliberately amplified to give governments an excuse to control the population (e.g., through the imposition of martial law). At the same time, as we saw above, a third category of conspiracy theory uses precisely the opposite reasoning to claim that the crisis is being *downplayed in the interests a powerful outgroup*. In particular, conspiracy theorists argue that governments and health officials have deliberately under-reported the extent of the crisis in order to avoid panic or to shore up the economy.

Responses to conspiracy theories need to address people's vulnerability, not alienate them further

There are a number of reasons to believe that there is little value in trying to change the mind of a conspiracy theorist with facts alone. For example, research on misinformation and rumours suggests that it is remarkably difficult to correct misconceptions (Lewandowsky, Ecker, Seifert, Schwarz, & Cook, 2012). Even if people do update their thinking in the face of correction, corrections can fade from memory over time, while the familiarity of the original myth lingers, potentially leading people to endorse it (again) despite the correction (Swire, Ecker, & Lewandowsky, 2017). For people who hold the conspiracist worldview, corrective information may be particularly ineffective. First, most conspiracy theorists already know the official version of events, so there is little point repeating it. Second, because the establishment is seen to be the source of misinformation and subterfuge, authorities' messages of reassurance are likely to fall on deaf ears. Indeed, the usual rules of persuasion – pointing out official facts and noting that there is consensus around the official version – can be inverted to be seen as *proof* of the conspiracy (e.g., an example of vested interests controlling the narrative). Third, many conspiracy theorists are psychologically wedded to the notion that something sinister is afoot, and fall prey to motivated reasoning and confirmation biases (Hornsey & Fielding, 2017). Conspiracy theorists refute disconfirming evidence or generate new theories to take the place of discredited ones, shifting goalposts in ways that seem fantastical, frustrating and hard to follow. Because of this, you can never really disprove a conspiracy theory.

So what advice might we have for leaders who want to respond to conspiracy theories? Well, first, resist the temptation to use conspiracist language oneself.

If leaders fall into the habit of using conspiracy theories to wage intergroup battles, then they may find it hard to put that genie back in the bottle when the conspiracy theories turn on them. Beyond that, leaders need to communicate through both words *and action* that they are operating with integrity, and doing their best to assuage feelings of mistrust, powerlessness, and alienation that provide the breeding ground for conspiracist thinking. Indeed, there is evidence that priming feelings of control in the laboratory can reduce people's belief in conspiracy theories (van Prooijen & Acker, 2015). Responding to these feelings of vulnerability might be a more effective way of defeating conspiracy theories than repeating evidence alone.

This is an essential 'long-game' that leaders need to play in winning the psychological battle over COVID-19. Although a degree of healthy scepticism about official accounts of events is to be encouraged, *chronic* scepticism becomes a problem, as people ignore facts and resist advice. Now is a time to be listening to our scientists and to our government officials, not to be casting them as colluders, manipulators, and liars. And for leaders, now is the time to build social identification, not to undermine it.

SECTION

C
SOCIAL (DIS)-CONNECTEDNESS

A disaster (which originally meant 'ill-starred', or 'under a bad star') changes the world and our view of it. Our focus shifts, and what matters shifts. What is weak breaks under new pressure, what is strong holds, and what was hidden emerges. Change is not only possible, we are swept away by it. We ourselves change as our priorities shift, as intensified awareness of mortality makes us wake up to our own lives and the preciousness of life. Even our definition of 'we' might change as we are separated from schoolmates or co-workers, sharing this new reality with strangers. Our sense of self generally comes from the world around us, and right now, we are finding another version of who we are. (Solnit, 2020)

As Rebecca Solnit eloquently observes, COVID-19 has changed our lives in profound ways. We outlined in Section A how our identities are defined in substantial part by the groups to which we belong. It follows that if we are separated from these groups, then our sense of self can be profoundly shaken. In this section, we turn our attention to some of the precursors and consequences of social disconnection.

The section opens with an examination of COVID-19's capacity to *threaten* not just us personally but also our group memberships, and hence our social identities (Chapter 7). This is followed by a discussion of the ways in which *risk is perceived* through the lens of group membership (Chapter 8). Our focus then pivots to exploring the consequences of COVID-19 for mental health and well-being. We start by examining how the *social isolation* that results from quarantine policies can lead to loneliness (Chapter 9) before zeroing in on *ageing and connectedness* (Chapter 10). The section concludes by looking at COVID-19 as a form of *collective trauma*, and considering how group processes affect people's resilience in the face of the virus (Chapter 11). Together, these considerations serve to highlight two key points: first, apart from the physical effects of the virus itself, COVID-19 is also a hazard to health by virtue of the threat it poses to people's social identities; second, these social identities and those that emerge in the context of a pandemic are a key resource that is critical to the protection and promotion of health.

7

Group Threat

Katharine H. Greenaway

The biggest threat to the Territory is clear. It is not us, it's them.

(Western Australian Premier, Mark McGowan)

We live in a dangerous world. In addition to threats from terrorism, climate change and natural disasters, our sense of danger has become particularly acute as the globe reels in the face of a once-in-a-century pandemic. While the threat may feel unprecedented, people's reactions to it are not. Indeed, there are remarkable similarities between the ways that people react to threats of various forms and the ways that our group memberships affect our experiences of those threats.

A crisis has a profound effect on the ways in which we draw lines between ourselves and others: between strangers and family, between rivals and allies, and between foreigners and fellow citizens. Whether we draw these lines inclusively or exclusively, one feature of the COVID-19 crisis is that it has brought into sharp focus the groups to which we belong: our families, our local community, our country. As we noted in Section A, this means that such threats are generally associated with a heightened sense of *shared social identity*, such that our sense of self is defined to a greater extent by those group memberships. In these times of uncertainty, there is also an enhanced need to understand what being a member of these groups entails and how we should act. How best can I look after my family? What is an appropriate community response? What should 'we' ('we parents', 'we practitioners', 'we progressives') be doing?

This chapter addresses these questions and explores how the threat posed by COVID-19 affects our sense of connection to groups, with a focus on how different framings of this threat have different consequences for the group. In particular, research points to important differences between threats that originate from *outside* one's own ingroup (i.e., a between-group, or intergroup threat) and threats that originate from *within* one's own ingroup (a within-group, or intragroup threat). While intergroup threats tend to increase solidarity, trust and cooperation, intragroup threats tend to undermine such responses (Greenaway & Cruwys, 2019). Although threat has the potential to undermine a collective response to the pandemic, it can also be shaped in ways that promote social solidarity during this tumultuous time. These are the issues this chapter explores in the context of COVID-19.

Threats from within an ingroup can undermine solidarity, trust and cooperation

The nature of an infectious disease, especially one that can spread from asymptomatic carriers, is that it is often our close contacts and loved ones who are the source of the threat – meaning that the virus can be understood as an intragroup threat. In the case of COVID-19, it is apparent that some public health messages inadvertently encourage us to be suspicious of our friends, neighbours and fellow citizens, calling on us to assume that they have the disease and are spreading it among us. This has the effect of undermining group ties, as evidenced by a study that investigated threat in the context of Ebola infection (Greenaway & Cruwys, 2015). The study found that US citizens who read about a case of Ebola on US soil identified less strongly as Americans when the case was described as a *US citizen* than when it was described as a *Sierra Leone citizen*. Such de-identification can be understood to reflect people's inclination to 'psychologically exit' a group that is under threat, and is especially common among group members who were not strongly committed to the group in the first place (Spears, Doosje, & Ellemers, 1997). If this inclination toward psychological exit becomes a dominant response, it can lead the group to fracture (Sani, 2008).

Such processes are undoubtedly a barrier to effectively combatting the threats posed by COVID-19. In fighting the virus, people around the world are required to embark upon unprecedented levels of behaviour change that most view as unpleasant. If they do not identify with others, they are unlikely to embark on such change. Furthermore, if an intragroup threat weakens the social fabric of groups, this prevents people from accessing the psychological resources associated with group membership (of a form set out in Chapter 2). For example, if a person does not identify with their neighbours, they are unlikely to go to them for support – even if they are in dire need of it.

Threats from outside the group can bolster solidarity, trust and cooperation

Given the potential divisiveness that can ensue when COVID-19 is framed as an intragroup threat, it is perhaps not surprising that many world leaders have instead sought to frame COVID-19 as an intergroup threat: as a 'foreign' disease spread by outsiders. Intergroup threats tend to strengthen people's commitment to their ingroup (e.g., Castano, Yzerbyt, Paladino, & Sacchi, 2002; Ellemers, Spears, & Doosje, 1997). For instance, following the 9/11 attacks on the Twin Towers, American university students' identification with their country increased relative to a baseline taken six months prior (Moskalenko, McCauley, & Rozin, 2006). This in turn makes a difference to people's behaviour. For instance, social identification enhances people's trust in fellow group members (Cruwys, Greenaway et al., 2020) as well as their willingness to cooperate in working towards group goals (Haslam, 2001). We have witnessed this in the context of the COVID-19 crisis. As the emergency developed, there was an outpouring of collective solidarity in all parts of the world, as evidenced by the 'Adopt a Healthcare Worker' campaign and a surge in volunteerism (United Nations, 2020). In many parts of the world this elevated concern for the well-being of one's fellow citizens has also been reflected in expanded government welfare policies, with even Conservative governments introducing income guarantees that would have been considered radically progressive in previous years (van Leeuwen, 2020).

While leaders may frame COVID-19 as an intergroup threat in order to encourage citizens to respond collectively, this can also have negative consequences for intergroup relations. Indeed, a large body of work has found that the perception of intergroup threat increases intolerance, prejudice and punishment of outgroup members (e.g., McCann, 2008; Skitka, Bauman, Aramovich, & Morgan, 2006). Unfortunately, intergroup threat can also inspire hostile and punitive reactions, even towards targets that have no objective link with the threat in question. For example, acts of racism towards people of Asian appearance spread across the world even faster than COVID-19 itself (Shimizu, 2020; see Chapter 19).

Inclusive social identities can attenuate perceived threats to an ingroup

It is clear that both intragroup and intergroup threats have unique downsides. While intergroup threat can increase feelings of ingroup identification and ingroup solidarity, it also sharpens the boundaries of who is inside and who is outside the group, triggering greater prejudice towards the latter. Conversely, intragroup threat may not directly cause outgroup hostility, but it can undermine ingroup solidarity and cohesion. In turn, this can lead people not only to seek out less group-based social support, but also to provide less support to other ingroup members who are in need.

How, then, can we frame a threat like COVID-19 to harness the benefits of intergroup threat without also suffering the negative consequences? There are several approaches to mitigating the downsides of group threat. One that is particularly promising involves framing COVID-19 as an intergroup threat in which the outgroup is not another nation or community of people but rather the *virus itself* (see Figure 5, and also Section D). Such an approach seeks to emphasise our common humanity as an expanded shared ingroup and has been found to improve intergroup attitudes (Wohl & Branscombe, 2005; see also Chapter 20).

Another approach to preventing the downsides of group threat involves helping people to feel more secure while being buffeted by the winds of fate. More specifically, people need to feel in control (Gerber & Wheeler, 2009). If people feel that they have the capacity to control important outcomes in the face of a threat to their group, they are less likely to react with hostility and outgroup prejudice (Greenaway, Louis, Hornsey, & Jones, 2014).

This sense of control can also be collective in nature. Indeed, research suggests that when we believe that our *group* has control of a situation, this can contribute to a sense of personal control, and also help to promote effective responses to threat (Fritsche et al., 2013). In the context of group threats such as COVID-19, messages by governments and health organisations are therefore critical in reassuring individuals that the situation is generally under control. Here, the most effective messages are those that not only provide people with ways to gain control, but also tie this to important group goals. The slogan 'Stay Home. Save Lives' is a good example of this (*Otago Daily Times*, 2020).

However, if governments and authorities fail to provide clear messages, they can exacerbate people's sense that they lack control, and this in turn can intensify negative group-based reactions to the threat. Indeed, poor (or mixed) messaging of this form has been identified as a persistent problem in both the United States (Bennett, 2020) and Brazil (Phillips, 2020). As New York's governor, Andrew Cuomo, observed, 'That confusion … adds to the fear and the frustration of people because if [the] government doesn't know what it's doing, then people feel they're really alone and this is really a problem' (Bennett, 2020).

In summary, it is clear that authorities' messaging is critical in guiding people's reactions to group threat. Governments and global health organisations have a vitally important role to play in crafting messages that will determine how people perceive and react to the threat posed by COVID-19. The tone they set has the potential to bring people together in a common spirit to respond collectively and effectively (in ways we discussed in Section B). However, if misjudged, these messages have the potential to unleash a wave of distrust

Figure 5   Pathogen resistance

directed towards other ingroup members or outgroup members. As we highlight in various chapters in this book, getting this right requires leadership that engenders a sense of common fate and encourages people to join in cooperative efforts to defeat the virus both locally and globally. Indeed, as Figure 5 suggests, this is COVID-19's worst nightmare.

8

Risk Perception

Tegan Cruwys

Patient A1.1, who was then still experiencing mild respiratory symptoms, attended a birthday party with nine other people. They hugged and shared food at the three-hour party. Seven of the attendees soon became ill. Within about a week of the onset of symptoms, the condition of [patient A1.1] deteriorated. The person was hospitalized, put on a ventilator and subsequently died. . . . Meanwhile, two of the birthday party attendees became critically ill and were put on ventilators. Both died. (Cha, 2020)

The behaviours that cause – or prevent – the spread of COVID-19 are 'micro' behaviours that people engage in dozens of times every day: touching one's face, shaking hands, physically distancing from other customers in the supermarket, or visiting an ageing relative. These behaviours ultimately determined whether a community managed to 'flatten the curve' and become one of the success stories in the initial COVID-19 response, or alternatively, experienced uncontrolled spread and ensuing tragedy. However, there is rarely complete alignment between the perceived risk of these behaviours and their actual risk. This complicates the goal of minimising those interactions that are high risk for transmission (e.g., large intergenerational family gatherings with shared food) without banning those activities that are unlikely to pose a risk (e.g., going for a solo run on a quiet beach).

Shared group membership attenuates risk perception and increases health risk taking

As outlined in Section A, when people see themselves and others through the lens of social identities, their behaviour, emotions, and thoughts are fundamentally shaped by these social identities. It should come as no surprise, then, that one of the things affected by shared group membership is our perception of risk. The first evidence that social relationships affect health risk taking was documented by public health campaigners attempting to slow the spread of sexually transmitted diseases, particularly HIV. Researchers found that people were far less likely to take precautions (and were therefore far more likely to contract STDs) when their sexual partner was someone they trusted and had a close relationship with (Hammer, Fisher, Fitzgerald, & Fisher, 1996). Similarly, needle sharing is not a behaviour that occurs in a vacuum; instead it is most likely to occur in small, tight-knit groups of users among whom there is reciprocal trust (Unger et al., 2006).

The evidence that these processes are driven by social identity has been gathered primarily in the context of mass gatherings. For decades, mass gatherings have been seen as major sites for the spread of contagious disease (Tam et al., 2012). Indeed, pilgrimages to Qom in Iran have been implicated in the global spread of COVID-19 (Memish, Ahmed, Schlagenhauf, Doumbia, & Khan, 2020). Mass gatherings also present heightened health risks associated with poor sanitation, hardships such as extreme weather and noise, and limited capacity for help in emergencies, because emergency services often have great difficulty accessing crowded areas (Ranse et al., 2017). However, attendees typically do not perceive mass gatherings as risky places. This is because people use shared group membership with others as a heuristic, or proxy indicator, for safety. Social identity researchers have found that the more strongly people identify with fellow attendees at a mass gathering, the more likely they are to report *comfort* and well-being in these environments (Cruwys et al., 2019; Novelli, Drury, & Reicher, 2010) and the less likely they are to be disturbed by the risks posed by the crowd (Pandey, Stevenson, Shankar, Hopkins, & Reicher, 2013).

Experimental evidence also speaks to the capacity for shared group membership to attenuate perceptions of disease risk. In one 'minimal group' study, 123 participants were randomly assigned to a red group or a green group, and asked to finish building a Lego model commenced by a previous participant. They encountered dirty tissues in the shared workspace that were attributed to a previous participant with a cold. Participants showed greater concern about the risk to their own health when the previous participant was identified as an outgroup member than as an ingroup member (Cruwys, Greenaway, et al., 2020). Critically for the COVID-19 context, these findings are not specific to perception but also extend to actual behaviour. For example,

Firing and Laberg (2012) found that military officers were more likely to participate in a collective and risky leap into ocean waters when they identified strongly with their fellow officers. Indeed, social factors more strongly predicted this behaviour than did officers' personal characteristics (e.g., their impulsivity).

In summary, social identity processes will have a dual role in shaping risk perception during the COVID-19 pandemic. On the one hand, they can support accurate assessment of risk (e.g., leading people to not sit near a stranger on public transport). On the other hand, they can also compromise them (e.g., so that people share a meal with friends or hug a relative).

Shared group membership facilitates trust and attenuates disgust

Why do we see this link between shared group membership and willingness to engage in risky health behaviours? Studies have found evidence for two pathways: a cognitive pathway related to *trust* and an emotional pathway related to *disgust*. Let us look at these in turn.

The link between trust and risk taking is well established. For example, a series of experimental studies using investment and gambling games found that people will take more risks (in this case, invest more money) when the outcomes of a game are controlled by someone they trust (e.g., Cook et al., 2014). Indeed, even when group membership was randomly determined on the basis of arbitrary criteria, people were still more likely to trust ingroup members than outgroup members to take care of their interests (Tanis & Postmes, 2005). These processes also play a role in risk taking that can lead to disease transmission. In one study with over 350 participants, people were asked to consider a scenario in which their work colleague, without asking permission, took a sip from the participant's own cup of coffee (Cruwys, Greenaway, et al., 2020). The work colleague was described as either sharing nationality with the participant or as being a foreigner. Participants trusted the colleague less in the latter case, perceiving there to be a greater risk to their health after sharing drinks. Consistent with a social identity interpretation of these effects, this effect was most pronounced among people who strongly identified with their nation.

Disgust constitutes a second pathway through which shared group membership can affect health-risk perceptions and behaviour. Although disgust might be unpleasant, it is an adaptive emotion that specifically evolved to motivate us to avoid things likely to pose a risk of disease: spoiled food, waste products, and bodily secretions (Curtis, de Barra, & Aunger, 2011). Extending this to group contexts, on evolutionary grounds, one can predict that such a disgust response extends towards outgroup members to protect us from new diseases (Murray & Schaller, 2016). That is, for much of human history, different groups interacted rarely and contact with new groups was sometimes devastating, as infectious diseases spread rapidly among immunologically naïve populations. For example, the colonisation of the Americas likely enabled the spread of syphilis through Europe and, even more devastatingly, the spread of smallpox through North America (Ramenofsky, Wilbur, & Stone, 2003).

While disgust is heightened for outgroup members, there is evidence that it is lower for those whom we see as ingroup members. Returning to the context of mass gatherings, two studies by Hult Khazaie and Khan (2019) found that people who felt a sense of shared identity with fellow attendees felt less disgust towards these ingroup members, and less vulnerable to the risk of disease. These findings have been corroborated by experimental evidence. For instance, one study found that participants who were asked to handle a sweaty t-shirt felt more disgust and walked faster to clean their hands when the t-shirt belonged to an outgroup member than when it belonged to an ingroup member (Reicher, Templeton, Neville, Ferrari, & Drury, 2016).

Integrating group processes into public health messaging will improve their effectiveness

In a COVID-19 context, these various processes can have ironic effects. Because distrust and disgust are lower for ingroup than outgroup members, people might be more likely to engage in behaviours that risk disease transmission *specifically* when interacting with people whom they perceive to be ingroup members. It has been clear from the beginning of the COVID-19 outbreak that most transmission occurs within the context of families or other communal gatherings (e.g., birthday parties, weddings), rather than through contact with strangers or foreigners (Cha, 2020). For this reason, 'othering' the disease, as a problem caused or experienced by outgroups (see also Chapters 7 and 19), misrepresents who the most likely vectors are – those with whom we *feel* safe. This also leads us to take risks that we otherwise would not. Stark evidence for this is provided by Australian data on people's compliance with recommended physical distancing measures (collected in April 2020; Liddy, Hanrahan, & Byrd, 2020). While an impressive 84% of people avoided strangers on public transport, only 54% of people avoided colleagues or their workplace. A mere 13% of people reduced physical contact with those in their home.

Public health messaging needs to take account of these social identity dynamics. In particular, it needs to engage with the fact that people's desire to keep ingroup members safe is at odds with the fact that they are slow to recognise the risks that ingroup members pose to health. A key way to do this is by emphasising that physical distance is an *act of care* towards other group members, not a sign of mistrust.

9

Social Isolation

Sarah V. Bentley

They had been sentenced, for an unknown crime, to an indeterminate period of punishment. (Camus, *The Plague*, 1947, p. 92)

As Camus observed in *The Plague*, quarantine is more than just 'staying home' – it feels like a punishment, and can take a significant toll on people's health. The impact of social disconnection on both quality of life and lifespan has long been known. In particular, pioneering research by Berkman and Syme (1979) found that people who lacked social contact lived far shorter lives than those who were well connected, even when controlling for other obvious determinants of longevity, such as physical health, health behaviours (e.g., smoking), and use of health services.

In less morbid epidemiological research, Cohen and colleagues found that people with more diverse social networks were in fact significantly less susceptible to the common cold (Cohen, Doyle, Turner, Alper, & Skoner, 2003). Indeed, among people exposed to the common cold, the least sociable were twice as likely to become ill as the most sociable. More recently still, a meta-analysis of studies including more than 300,000 people (Holt-Lunstad, Smith, & Layton, 2010) found that the effect of social isolation on life expectancy was comparable with the effects of smoking. But it is not only physical health that is impacted by a lack of social connection. Research has also shown that the association between social isolation and health is particularly strong for mental health, with robust associations with depression, anxiety, and substance use (e.g., Ingram et al., 2020).

Though many people may have previously been unaware of social isolation's adverse effects (Haslam, McMahon et al., 2018), these may now have been brought home by their personal experiences of living under lockdown conditions. Moreover, as isolation became the norm rather than the exception, so too did its health consequences. Indeed, Google registered a global spike in searches for 'isolation' and 'loneliness' beginning in mid-February 2020 (Google Trends, 2020). At the same time, suicide-crisis phone lines around the world reached their highest ever demand (Neal, 2020). In the face of COVID-19 restrictions, many people who have never experienced significant mental health difficulties before have found themselves struggling with insomnia, anxiety, and emotion dysregulation for the first time.

In this context, one important question to ask is whether the link between social isolation and ill-health is merely an association, or whether feeling isolated *causes* poor health. This issue was explored in a series of studies prior to the COVID-19 outbreak. For example, one study followed a large and representative sample of over 21,000 New Zealanders across a five-year period, tracking changes in their social connectedness and mental health (Saeri, Cruwys, Barlow, Stronge, & Sibley, 2018). People who experienced a drop in their degree of social connectedness were at elevated risk of a decline in their mental health one year later. The relationship also went the other way: people who experienced a decline in their mental health tended to become more isolated one year later. Importantly, though, the former relationship was about three times stronger than the latter. This suggests that people are more likely to lose social connections prior to mental health decline, rather than the other way around.

Interestingly, we are better able to respond to the challenges that life throws our way when we simply reflect on our social connections – in particular, on the social groups that we belong to. In one experiment, prior to completing an unsolvable problem-solving task, half of the participants were asked to reflect on the many groups to which they belonged, while the other half were not. When faced with failure on the task, the former participants were subsequently less distressed. This points to the capacity for valued group memberships to protect mental health in trying circumstances (Cruwys, South, Greenaway, & Haslam, 2015).

Critically, what this large body of evidence indicates is that the extended and widespread period of social isolation brought about by the COVID-19 lockdown is likely to have a significant and serious impacts on health, especially mental health. Our goal here is not to question the medical necessity of stay-at-home orders, or their role in reducing demand on hospitals. Instead, we seek to highlight that there are also public health *costs* of such a policy, particularly for mental health. Crucially, we also illustrate how the negative effects of social isolation might be mitigated, which is of enduring relevance not only during the COVID-19 crisis but also in building an inclusive and healthy society in its aftermath.

Isolation will hit some harder than others

A large body of research has examined people's capacity to navigate significant life changes – for example, those associated with parenthood, retirement, and entry into higher education. In every case, findings suggest that positive connections to others are a source of psychological resilience that helps people negotiate the transition successfully (Haslam, Haslam, Jetten, Cruwys, & Steffens, 2020). However, unlike most life changes, COVID-19 has required people to drastically reduce social contact to combat the pandemic. This is likely to have been particularly disruptive to people's capacity to maintain social connections and hence their ability to cope with the challenges the virus presents. One particular group at elevated risk is older people (the focus of Chapter 10). More worryingly still, those whose level of social connection was already low prior to COVID-19 are at heightened risk of severe isolation, and its negative health consequences. Indeed, it is clear that the pandemic has disrupted the fragile circumstances of millions of people already living with challenges such as mental illness, domestic violence, or homelessness. For example, within a month of physical distancing measures being put in place, countries around the world saw a spike in demand for social services such as domestic violence support (Taub, 2020).

Data collected in late March 2020 with 536 UK residents shows that the pandemic situation is much more difficult for those already at risk (Bentley, Cruwys, Jetten, Crimston, & Selvanathan, 2020). At this time, people in the UK were experiencing the phased introduction of physical distancing, but had not yet gone into full lockdown. The survey focused on key outcomes that are essential not only to the people experiencing the challenges of COVID-19, but also to those trying to lead them through it: access to knowledge, preparedness for self-isolation, feelings of trust, and a sense of community cohesion. People with the lowest levels of social support were those least likely to rate their access to information as adequate, to feel that others were behaving responsibly, or to feel that their community was cohesive. They were also more likely to express concern about their capacity to cope with self-isolation. By contrast, those who reported feeling more connected to others consistently reported having more trust and better access to relevant information, and felt their community was more cohesive. Most dramatically, those who were in the loneliest 10% of the sample were *eight times* more likely to report clinical levels of psychological distress than those in the least lonely 10% of the sample.

We can only be 'together apart' by building community and belonging

In order to understand how people can stay together while apart, it is important to consider why social isolation proves to be such a powerful trigger for ill health. The answer lies in the key insight that humans are fundamentally social beings who derive a sense of self (and everything that goes with it, such as self-worth and self-efficacy) from their group memberships. The social identities we derive from our group memberships allow us to leverage social support and furnish us with a sense of purpose and control – all critical resources for our health (Jetten, Haslam, Haslam, Dingle, & Jones, 2014). This means that social activities are not simply an 'optional extra'. Rather, in allowing us to live out our social identities, groups are crucial to healthy psychological functioning. For example, it is not enough to merely attend a choir rehearsal to reap the benefits of being a chorister. Instead, you need to feel a sense of *belonging* to your choir. Many recommendations for how to stay connected miss the mark because they do not focus on the central role of social identities. Some are preoccupied with the *medium* of social contact, for instance, in emphasising the need for face-to-face or video contact, rather than phone or message-based contact. Other misguided advice risks a preoccupation with the *amount* of social contact, imploring people to have daily contact or else risk a decline in well-being. What both such recommendations miss is an understanding of the psychology of isolation. A social identity perspective instead reveals that the crucial 'ingredient' in social relationships that makes them so beneficial for health resides in neither the format nor the dosage. Instead, it is the subjective sense of belonging to some greater collective that is crucial. To the extent that people feel that they remain connected to meaningful communities during lockdown – either through virtual or other means – they will be relatively protected (see also Chapter 10).

Given what we know about the risks of isolation and who will be most affected, the critical question is therefore that of what can be done to reduce the impact of stay-at-home orders, especially for those who are most vulnerable. The most important principle is that physical distance does not preclude social connection. Modern technology enables people to stay connected without risking infection in ways that would have been impossible even 10 years ago. Indeed, this insight contributed to the World Health Organization's decision to drop the term 'social distancing' (Greenaway, Saeri, & Cruwys, 2020).

Structured interventions may also be able to help people stay connected. Prior to the COVID-19 pandemic, social identity researchers had developed an intervention known as Groups 4 Health (G4H) to address social isolation. Importantly, G4H has been evaluated in randomised controlled trials and shown to reduce loneliness, depression and anxiety (Haslam, Cruwys, et al., 2019). However, G4H is a face-to-face programme, and in the world of COVID-19 this makes it hard to implement. Interventions such as this must therefore be adapted to suit a remote context. Groups 2 Connect is an online adaptation of G4H that raises awareness of the impact of connectedness, and focuses realistically on what people can do within physical distancing requirements to maintain a sense of connection to others. Initial evidence suggests that, like G4H, this is beneficial for connectedness and well-being.

More generally, the pandemic has produced some heart-warming examples of people maintaining community despite isolation. People singing together from their apartment balconies in densely populated areas of both Wuhan and Milan (Taylor, 2020); online cooking classes connecting people to their cultural heritage; orchestras and bands co-producing rousing anthems from separated sites (Asprou, 2020; Lam, 2020). There are also reports of a huge growth in neighbourhood-based social media groups, as well as a global rise in cooperative online gaming (Moody, 2020). Each of these examples showcases innovative solutions to the problem of remaining connected. They also speak to the fact that while groups have historically been portrayed as toxic, the data actually suggest that the opposite is true. It would seem that protecting people against the toxic effects of isolation needs to centre on the key thing that they are being denied – meaningful group-based connection. Indeed, finding ways to be *together apart* needs to be a core part of the COVID-19 response.

10

Ageing and Connectedness

Catherine Haslam

In order to reduce the spread of the virus and to protect vulnerable persons, it is strongly advised to reduce physical contact, not to visit older persons, not to go to care homes and nursing homes. (European Federation of Psychologists' Associations [EFPA], 2020)

This statement by the EFPA is one of many recommendations that emerged in March 2020 as the health consequences of COVID-19 were being recognised internationally. In many countries, the restrictions imposed to limit the spread of the virus have seemed particularly severe for older people, due to concerns about their greater vulnerability and risk of serious illness and death. Let us be in no doubt, the advice to physically distance from one another has been an essential public health policy for protecting older people from COVID-19. But, as the previous chapter outlined, its unintentional consequence – of increasing social disconnection and loneliness – is a recognised health hazard that itself requires careful management. This chapter focuses on the particular challenges of isolation for older people as well as potential solutions.

Older people are at particular risk of poor health due to isolation

Perhaps counterintuitively, recent national surveys indicated that prior to COVID-19, older people were some of the *least* lonely in society (Haslam,

Haslam, & Cruwys, 2019). At first sight, we might imagine this would be advantageous when it comes to combating the threat of social disconnection posed by the pandemic. However, things are not that simple, for social connections can only act as resources to bolster health and well-being when they are *accessible* and when they provide a vehicle to *maintain and extend* meaningful ties. Under conditions of lockdown, the primary means through which people connect are virtual and hence rely on technology, which is often less accessible to older people because it is unfamiliar or unaffordable. If this is the case, then older people stand to lose their social connection 'advantage'. Furthermore, some countries have proposed 'shielding' older people by imposing lockdown measures only for these people – meaning their isolation is likely to be longer and more extreme than that of other groups.

This is all the more concerning because, if they become disconnected, older people are more susceptible to the health risks associated with loneliness. Indeed, evidence shows that older people living with chronic loneliness visit their physician more often, are more likely to require rehospitalisation, and more often develop multiple chronic illnesses than their more connected counterparts (Gerst-Ermerson & Jayawardhana, 2015). They also experience greater and more rapid decline in cognitive health, mobility and mental health than those who do not feel lonely (Kuiper et al., 2015). These widespread effects across all domains of health have been attributed to the ways in which chronic loneliness compromises the immune system over time (Hawkley & Cacioppo, 2003), predisposing lonely people to new illnesses as well as intensifying any pre-existing conditions.

From this substantial evidence base, we can predict that a major 'shock' to the social support system such as the COVID-19 pandemic is likely to have more serious consequences for the mental, physical and cognitive health of older adults. Moreover, where chronic loneliness emerges as a consequence of physical distancing restrictions, this will increase the likelihood of negative health outcomes (e.g., increased falls, more rapid cognitive decline) that limit a person's capacity to live independently.

Gaining group ties mitigates the health costs of loneliness for older people

The obvious way to counteract these adverse health consequences is by striving to sustain or, if possible, to build social connection. The science is also clear about the form that these connections should take – they must be meaningful, preferably multiple, and include social groups (Haslam, Jetten, et al., 2018). This is evidenced by three studies which draw on the English Longitudinal Study of Ageing, a population survey with multiple waves of data from more than 18,000 people aged 50+ living in the community. The first showed that older adults who lost two social group memberships following retirement had a 12% risk of mortality over the next six years (Steffens, Cruwys, Haslam, Jetten, & Haslam, 2016). However, this risk fell to just 2% if people were able to maintain their group memberships, and to less than 1% if people gained groups in the post-retirement period.

The second study compared the effects of different forms of social engagement on cognitive integrity over three time points each separated by two years (Haslam, Cruwys, & Haslam, 2014). This found that group-based ties offer benefits for cognitive health, even after one-on-one social ties were accounted for. Furthermore, as Figure 6 shows, the group ties became even more important for cognitive health as people got older.

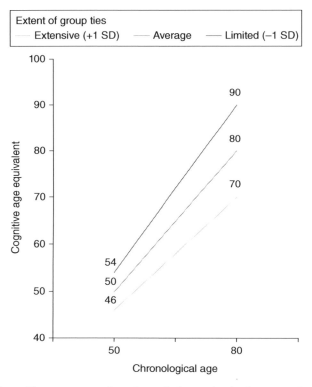

Figure 6 Cognitive age as a function of chronological age and extent of social group ties

The third study looked at the benefits of group memberships for mental health among older people with a history of depression (Cruwys et al., 2013). On average, people who have experienced depression will go on to have between five and nine separate depressive episodes in their lifetime (Burcusa & Iacono, 2007), which points to the difficulty of achieving stable long-term recovery. However, Cruwys and colleagues (2013) show that joining groups can play a critical role in protecting people against relapse. In particular, they found that people with depression who joined three or more groups within two years had only a 15% risk of depression relapse six years later. This compared to a 41% risk of relapse for those who joined no groups over this period.

These population studies are backed up by evidence from experimental and intervention studies among older people living in care, which illustrate that acquiring positive group memberships (e.g., through a social club or reminiscence group) is causally linked to better mental, cognitive and physical health (Gleibs et al., 2011; Knight, Haslam, & Haslam, 2010). Importantly, these effects do not arise from joining just *any* group. Rather, the data show that it is only those groups that get 'under a person's skin' and become an important part of their sense of self that have this power. In other words, groups are only beneficial when people identify strongly with them (Haslam, Haslam, et al., 2014).

Nonetheless, like most other research in this area, this evidence of the benefits of group connectedness has been collected in contexts where people have been able to interact in close proximity. This therefore raises a key question in the COVID-19 era – can the health-related benefits of social connection still be harnessed when people are required to be physically separated from each other?

Technology can keep older people connected

More than ever, and particularly in the context of the COVID-19 pandemic, social interactions are increasingly dependent on technology. However, this shift to technology has been most prevalent in younger people. Evidencing this 'digital divide', prior to COVID-19, people under the age of 40 spent more time interacting via social media than face-to-face, whereas the opposite was true for those over 40 (Hall, 2018). With this in mind, a large number of studies have sought to investigate older people's use of technology, with many showing that this can have benefits for well-being, not least by increasing their sense of connection to other individuals and to society more broadly.

Unsurprisingly, these efforts are more successful when older people are *trained* to use technology (Delello & McWhorter, 2015) or technology is adapted to make it more user-friendly (Morton et al., 2018). Even more important is investment in making virtual connection *meaningful*: interventions are most successful when older adults are supported to pursue their interests through live webcasting (Botner, 2018) and videoconferencing (Hilton, Levine, & Zanetis, 2019).

However, social connection proves more challenging when people have neither the resources nor the confidence to use technology. While this can be ameliorated with resources and time, the speed with which COVID-19 restrictions were implemented allowed little time to address accessibility barriers for older people. Of course, there are other ways to connect with family and friends (e.g., through regular phone calls) and with neighbours (e.g., by interacting at a safe distance), but these often require resourcefulness, initiative and confidence – traits that can be compromised by the very fact of isolation. It is for precisely this reason that working with older adults to help them retain group-based connections is so important. Finding the best way to do this is a challenge in a pandemic, but it needs to be a priority.

11

Collective Trauma

Orla Muldoon

A traumatic event is one in which a person experiences a genuine fear of death or injury for themselves or others. Psychological symptoms in response to extreme and traumatic experiences are not unusual, and are captured under the umbrella term of *post-traumatic stress* (PTS). These can include disturbing thoughts and feelings long after the traumatic event has ended, feelings of detachment from others, hypervigilance to threat, and avoidance of reminders of the traumatic event. If symptoms are sufficiently intense and long-lasting, this may warrant a clinical diagnosis of post-traumatic stress disorder (PTSD).

While a substantial minority of people experience intense post-traumatic symptoms, what is sometimes overlooked is that most people are robust in the face of traumatic experiences and display psychological *resilience*. Although COVID-19 is a traumatic event likely to cause widespread PTS, group-based processes can play a key role in mitigating the severity of this and ensuring a more resilient response. This is particularly likely to be the case when the traumatic experience that people face is a *collective* experience such as COVID-19. Unlike a traumatic event such as an assault, with COVID-19 the threat to life and safety is common to us all. Indeed, it is precisely because 'we are all in this together' that the *collective curse* of the virus could potentially pave the way to a *collective cure* – notably through people overcoming challenge by banding together.

The trauma of COVID-19 is amplified by social disconnection

It is clear that a pandemic fits the definition of a traumatic event, in so far as it threatens people's lives and the lives of others they care about. Furthermore, there is evidence from previous disease outbreaks that such crises are widely *perceived* as traumatic. For instance, a review of the psychological impact of the 2003 SARS outbreak found consistent evidence that those affected experienced high levels of distress, and that this persisted for many years afterwards (Gardner & Moallef, 2015).

The requirement for people to self-isolate during the COVID-19 crisis is also likely to make it more traumatic. As discussed in previous chapters, this is because isolation disconnects people from each other and from meaningful groups that are a source of key social resources (e.g., social support; Haslam, Jetten, et al., 2018). There is evidence that quarantine measures amplify people's distress and compound the traumatic effects of an epidemic. For example, one study examined hospital employees in Beijing who were quarantined in 2003 due to SARS (Bai et al., 2004). It found that having been quarantined was the *most* important predictor of PTS symptoms. Similarly, adults and children who were quarantined due to SARS or the H1N1 outbreak in 2009 subsequently showed amplified levels of PTS symptoms (Braunack-Mayer, Tooher, Collins, Street, & Marshall, 2013). Another study indicated that the length of quarantine during the SARS outbreak also mattered. Specifically, those who were quarantined for more than 10 days were more likely to show PTSD symptoms than those quarantined for shorter periods (Hawryluck et al., 2004).

Group membership affects who is most vulnerable to traumatic stress in a pandemic

COVID-19 has connected the global community in an unprecedented fashion. While it is true that we are all in this together, the reality of the pandemic is that some groups are far more vulnerable than others. Indeed, group membership is a critical determinant of people's experience of the COVID-19 crisis – not only psychologically, as has been the focus of this volume, but also *structurally*. For instance, life in 2020 will be vastly different if you are a nurse rather than an academic, a New Yorker rather than a New Zealander, or aged 80 rather than 20. Moreover, those who cannot afford the luxuries of physical distancing, self-isolation or even running water and soap are made infinitely more vulnerable (Chung, Dong, & Li, 2020).

In many regards, these group-based realities mean that preventive actions are luxuries only those who live in more privileged circumstances can afford (in ways that we unpack further in Chapter 17). So, while the relatively well-off 'romanticise' the experience of quarantine (joking about their progress in learning to bake bread), others have to work in unsafe conditions where they cannot engage in physical distancing behaviours, or are in forced detainment where they cannot escape others. For the latter groups, not being able to self-isolate during a global pandemic may be especially traumatising. For those who cannot enact recommended safety behaviours or who are wilfully prevented from enacting them, advice to do so is alienating (see also Chapter 16 for how such experiences can lead to social disorder). Indeed, instructions to act in a way that is not feasible can increase anger and shatter a person's faith and trust in the world – experiences that are known to exacerbate PTS. Likewise, feelings of betrayal by the health and political system (that a person may have previously trusted), strongly predict more severe and lasting PTS symptoms (Muldoon et al., 2019).

However, *psychological* group memberships, both existing and emerging in the face of COVID-19, also affect people's vulnerabilities to traumatic stress. Indeed, when a person encounters a traumatic event, they are not a 'blank slate' but instead their response and ability to cope are shaped by their group memberships and the psychological resources that these provide. In this context, evidence suggests that the nature and number of a person's prior group memberships are important for at least two key reasons. First, pre-existing group memberships offer a platform for developing new connections that are likely to be crucial in helping them negotiate trauma and traumatic situations (Kinsella, Muldoon, Fortune, & Haslam, 2018). Second, those group memberships also provide group members with ongoing social connections that are the basis for social support as people negotiate trauma (Walsh, Muldoon, Gallagher, & Fortune, 2015). For example, people are more likely to find formal support services, such as counselling, more helpful when they are provided by others who are seen as ingroup members (Muldoon et al., 2019).

The collective nature of traumatic experience can support people's resilience

Although the scale and severity of COVID-related trauma will vary along group-based lines, many aspects of the experience are shared among members of the groups to which people belong. As a result, many people will have a sense that this major upheaval is a collective one, to be tackled collectively.

This is important because research suggests that the sharedness of traumatic experience is an important factor for mitigating the distress and anxiety that these events create (Kearns, Muldoon, Msetfi, & Surgenor, 2017). In particular, a sense of shared experience can contribute to feelings of collective efficacy (e.g., a shared perception that a community's collective efforts to flatten the curve are working). This in turn is likely to contribute to psychological resilience. Support for this hypothesis emerges from several lines of research. For example, in survey work among Nepalese survivors of a major earthquake, an emergent sense of identity with the devastated community was the basis for an enhanced sense of collective efficacy that predicted increased resilience (Muldoon et al., 2017). Furthermore, experimental work confirms that responses to a stressful situation are often driven by a *shared* understanding of the situation, and that this understanding has the power to suppress a physiological stress response in the face of challenge (Haslam & Reicher, 2006). Similarly, shared understandings of a traumatic situation have also been shown to attenuate its perceived stressfulness (Gallagher, Meaney, & Muldoon, 2014).

In short, a wealth of previous work suggests that there are likely to be multiple pathways through which group memberships will support people's resilience in the face of COVID-19. In particular, there is reason to believe that groups and associated social identities – both those which existed before the virus and those which have arisen as a result of the virus – will prove to be a key resource in mitigating the impact of traumatic stress. As Rebecca Solnit (2020) suggests in the article we quoted at the start of this section, one of the significant consequences of the pandemic has been the ability to appreciate anew not only the strength of our collective ties, but also their capacity to help us transform catastrophe into courage.

SECTION
D
COLLECTIVE BEHAVIOUR

We are frequently told that COVID-19 is the greatest challenge of our generation, and perhaps the largest global crisis since World War II. So, what do we know about how people behave in crises? And how can we apply that understanding to manage the current pandemic? The traditional answer draws on the notion that people are psychologically fragile at the best of times, and so threat and fear make things worse. This reasoning suggests that when you add collective psychology into the mix (either because we are actually in a crowd or because we see each other as all in the same boat) we simply fall apart. Panic turns a crisis into a disaster.

Despite the continuing popularity of this 'panic perspective', the evidence shows that, while people certainly can act selfishly and dysfunctionally in crises, more often they come together and support each other. An emergent collective psychology, far from being the villain of the piece, is what makes this possible. Living through the COVID-19 crisis is an experience we all have in common, and this has the potential to create a sense of shared identity which is the basis for mutual concern, mutual support, and resilience. In many ways, collective psychology is our greatest asset for dealing with a crisis.

It is critical for those dealing with the pandemic to appreciate the importance of this and to understand how to harness the benefits of collective psychology. This is true when it comes to fostering shared identity and solidarity not only *among* the public, but also *between* the public and authorities. Get it right and the rewards are considerable, not least because those authorities who treat the public as part of a common group are better able to guide the public to safety in a crisis. Get it wrong, however, and the costs are momentous. Error in this area not only creates tension between the public and the authorities, but also opens up divisions within communities and creates collective disorder.

In order to address these issues, this section starts with an outline of both traditional and contemporary models of *crowds* and collective behaviour (Chapter 12). Chapter 13 then outlines how people behave in *emergencies and disasters*, mapping the emergence of widespread solidarity. Chapter 14 explores the psychological underpinnings of *solidarity*, providing evidence for the critical role of shared social identity. Finally, the ways that different authorities can affect the development of shared identity is discussed in the final two chapters. Chapter 15 focuses on the emergency services and their relation with the public when *managing crowds in crises*. Chapter 16 looks at the nature of police–public encounters in determining *social order and disorder*. Overall, this section contains critical lessons for those managing the pandemic, because these factors determine not only how well we will deal with the crisis, but also what sort of society will emerge from it.

12

Crowds

Fergus Neville and Stephen D. Reicher

Crowds do not have a good reputation. They are associated with violence and excess, emotionality and irrationality – all summed up in the derisive word 'mob'. When people refer to 'mob psychology', the implications are always negative. The term is rooted in a contrast with refined, reasonable, and civilised behaviour. Above all, it implies a litany of loss: loss of reason, loss of restraint, loss of morality. In the mob, decent people become like beasts. It is therefore not surprising that in the midst of the COVID-19 crisis, aside from infection fears, gatherings of people on beaches, on public transport and in parks were met with concern and even alarm. Crowds are associated with trouble.

People have been taught to fear the masses as destructive forces

Crowd psychology emerged from concerns about the formation of a mass society in the era of industrialisation (Giner, 1976) and about the preservation of social order. At the root of such concerns lies a belief that in the absence of clear hierarchies to guide them, people are unable to think for themselves. This model holds that, given the psychological fragility of people and the futility of trying to reason with them, there is a need to shepherd them (see also Chapters 1 and 5).

If the masses were an imminent threat, the 'crowd' represented the moment at which they would rise up to batter down the social order. Hence the crowd has become a dense symbol of all that the elites feared in the mass: in the crowd, people were thought to be quintessentially destructive (Barrows, 1981). All these ideas were central in the writings of the early crowd psychologists: predominantly gentlemen scholars, particularly from France, which, in the Paris Commune of 1871, had witnessed the uprising and temporary victory of the masses. They had seen the crowd in action. They were terrified and haunted by it.

The most famous of those scholars was Gustave Le Bon. In his 1895 book *The Crowd*, Le Bon argues that the self is lost as one becomes submerged in the crowd. Loss of self means loss of standards, and so one has no means of evaluating and resisting the ideas and emotions to which one is exposed. These ideas therefore become 'contagious', spreading without check. Where do these ideas come from? Le Bon saw them as emerging from an atavistic collective unconscious which is exposed once the rational individual self has been stripped away. As a consequence, Le Bon asserted, crowd members are barbarians: fickle, emotional, unable to reason, sometimes heroic, but always destructive. It is not a pretty portrait. But it is an *influential* portrait, which continues to colour both popular views and the practices of agencies such as the police and emergency services (Drury, Novelli, & Stott, 2013), including those who report on and deal with mass behaviour in the COVID-19 crisis.

Crowd behaviour is shaped by shared notions of morality

Le Bon's portrait may be influential, but it is far from accurate. This is hardly surprising. He and his contemporaries viewed the crowd as horrified outsiders. Early crowd 'science' was a discipline rooted in fantasy and fear more than evidence (McPhail, 2017; Reicher, 2001). On closer and more systematic inspection a very different image emerges. Crowd events are not random explosions of rage. Indeed, violence and conflict are very much the exception rather than the rule (Barrows, 1981). But even in the most violent of crowds, behaviour remains orderly and patterned, and these patterns are socially meaningful (Davis, 1973).

Take food riots as an example (which many fear as a possible outcome of the COVID-19 pandemic; Paine, 2020; Thapar, 2020). One might think these to be the simplest of events: people get hungry, people see food, people get together and break down the doors to the stores, grab the food and run away. Yet, as Thompson (1971) shows in his analysis of nearly 700 such riots in England during the eighteenth century, the reality was very different. Riots typically happened when grain was being transported out of a locality. Crowds would 'confiscate' the sacks, sell them among themselves, return the money – and often the sacks as well – to the merchants. Not only was there a clear order to these 'riots', but people's behaviour also reflected what Thompson called a 'moral economy' among the peasant rioters. This refers to a collective understanding of rights and wrongs: that available resources should be distributed locally rather than being sent to market, and that they should be sold at a fair price.

Thompson's analysis also begins to explain what lies behind and produces crowd behaviour. The core of his argument is that people do not act, as Le Bon suggested, without standards and hence without constraint. Rather they act in terms of collective standards and shared notions of morality, which shape their actions. The key question for psychologists is how it is possible for collective beliefs to shape the behaviour of individuals in the crowd. The answer takes us back to the tenets of social identity theorising.

A social identity model of crowd action focuses on the shift from personal to social identity

We have seen how traditional crowd psychology views the crowd in entirely negative terms. And we have seen how, for Le Bon, this all starts in the loss of selfhood. For him, the individual self is the sole (valid) source of standards to guide our everyday behaviour. Loss of self therefore means the loss of any standards. It is here that the radical implications of the concept of social identity, as discussed in Chapter 2, become evident. The starting point of a social identity model of crowd action (Reicher, 1984, 1987) is that we do not lose identity, but rather *shift* from personal to social identity. Correspondingly, we do not lose standards, but rather the basis of our behaviour shifts from individual standards to collective norms, values and beliefs. As with Thompson's food rioters, crowd action has a social shape to the extent that crowd members are acting in terms of a common social identity characterised by a shared collective understanding.

In making this argument, we are not suggesting that any and every gathering of people develops a shared identity of this form. Shopping, commuting, sunbathing – there are many occasions where we may be physically crowded with others without having any sense of psychological connection to them. However, it is precisely by considering what happens when such a connection *does* emerge that we can begin to appreciate the implications of shared social identity in a crowd. We call this a psychological (as opposed to a physical) crowd.

Imagine yourself aboard a train crowded with strangers. You are psychologically distant from other individuals. Their chatter, their smell, and their touch as they press up against you are all odious. But then the train grinds to a halt. A loudspeaker announcement informs you, without much detail, that there is a problem. At this point, you begin to transition from separate individuals to a group of passengers bound together by common resentment against the rail company. As 'I' turns to 'we', the physical crowd transitions to a psychological crowd, and a series of other transitions occur (Neville, Novelli, Drury, & Reicher, in press).

First, there is the *cognitive* shift we have already described: people start to think in group terms. They relate to others as fellow group members rather than as strangers, and are motivated by their shared understanding of passenger rights. Second, there is a *relational* shift: people develop a greater intimacy with others, they start to turn and talk to each other, share revealing stories, and share their sandwiches. Such sharing and social support is vital in crises, as we outline in Chapters 13 to 15, and it generates a sense of empowerment, of mastery and of resilience (see Section C). This is particularly important when people have to endure difficult circumstances. Third, there is an *affective* shift. Intimacy, support and the sense of mastery are all pleasurable experiences. Together they mitigate the negatives of crisis situations, and perhaps explain why people can experience objectively trying conditions with a sense of subjective positivity (Hopkins et al., 2019).

Intergroup dynamics determine crowd behaviour

Thus far, we have concentrated mainly on the psychological transformation that occurs within a psychological crowd – the *intra*group dynamics. But crowd events are not just about the crowd. Typically, they involve more than one group – for example, fans of two rival sports teams, or protestors and counter-protestors, or, perhaps most frequently, the crowd and the police. No analysis of crowds is complete, therefore, without examining the processes that occur between groups – the *inter*group dynamics. This is particularly important if we want to understand how crowd conflict emerges (the topic of Chapters 16 and 18).

The key point is that violence and conflict do not inhere in the crowd in general, or even in the norms, values and beliefs of particular crowds (although some may be more or less opposed to the use of violence). Generally, it arises out of the interaction between multiple parties (Neville & Reicher, 2018). If one group is seen to be acting in ways that appear to threaten the other, or else to violate its sense of rights (either forcing them to do something they consider illegitimate or preventing them from doing something they consider legitimate), then this is likely to be contested, resulting in a spiral of tension that can culminate in violent conflict (Reicher, 1996). There are, of course, many different forms this can take. Where a community is divided among itself and particular minorities are accused of threatening the majority, it can lead to the type of pogroms described in Chapter 1 (see Reicher, Haslam, & Rath, 2008; also Chapters 19 and 20). Indeed, given that stigmatised groups are often considered dirty and diseased, this is particularly potent in a pandemic.

Crowds can be both destructive and constructive forces

It also follows that classic crowd theory is not just wrong about the nature of crowd action, it is actively misleading. In seeing crowds simply as a problem that must be eliminated, traditional thinking ignores the positive aspects of collective psychology – the solidarity and resilience that arise when people act with and for each other, and which are such an important resource in getting us through a crisis – and magnifies its negative aspects. The COVID-19 emergency has made it even more important to understand the constructive and avoid the destructive sides of crowds in a crisis. In the next chapter, we examine more closely exactly how people behave in an emergency.

13

Emergencies and Disasters

John Drury and Selin Tekin Guven

Over the last 50 years, we have come to know quite a lot about how people behave in emergencies and disasters. Using a variety of methods, research by sociologists and psychologists has identified a number of consistent features. This research has explored behaviour in diverse crises, such as fires, earthquakes, floods, storms and other natural hazards, as well as terrorist attacks. The COVID-19 crisis is different from these events in important ways. It comprises multiple incidents spread out over several months; and its effects are dispersed across the world rather than concentrated on a single group of people. Nevertheless, there are important similarities: there is a mortal threat, which can create fear; there is not enough protection for everyone under threat; and human action can mitigate (or exacerbate) that threat.

Understanding human behaviour in emergency events can therefore provide insights into behaviour during the COVID-19 pandemic. Nevertheless, some might ask why we need all that research. Don't we already know how people behave under conditions of mortal threat, inadequate protection and extreme fear? They panic!

What exactly do people mean by the term 'panic'? There are various definitions, but one thing that typically distinguishes the concept of 'panic' from related constructs, such as fear and flight, is the notion of *over-reaction*. It implies that the things people feel and the ways they act are *excessive*. A person suffering from panic has anxiety and fear reactions that are out of proportion with reality. So, to claim that people panic in an emergency is to claim that they over-react to the threat posed by the emergency.

What is more, the concept of panic incorporates an explanation for why people over-react. It is down to being in a crowd. Drawing on Le Bonian ideas (see Chapter 12), the supposition is that people have lost their minds, and the fear of each person 'infects' others through the process of contagion, heightening fear levels until they bear little relation to the original stimulus. But in an emergency, how do we establish whether fear is 'excessive'? At the time, there is generally so much uncertainty that it is impossible to know how significant the danger is. In retrospect it is easier to judge, because one can then sift the evidence to determine what was not known at the time.

For example, in the early days of the COVID-19 crisis, was the extra shopping that some people engaged in (so-called 'panic buying') necessarily excessive? By what criteria? If someone believes (a) that they may be forced to stay at home for an extended period in the near future, and/or (b) that other people will soon clear the shelves, then it makes perfect sense to buy extra oneself. It may be excessive from the perspective of the community, but not necessarily from the perspective of the actor (Luscombe, 2020). Most disaster researchers have therefore abandoned trying to judge whether behaviour in such events is rational or irrational, and have recommended focusing instead on what people do and why they do it.

Responses to danger are largely reasonable

In most emergencies, people need to respond urgently – usually by fleeing as quickly as possible. But instead, their response is often delayed. This is most evident in research on fires, but the same is also true for bombings and various natural hazards such as earthquakes, hurricanes and floods. In fact, it is this *under*-reaction, rather than 'panicked' *over*-reaction that is the major cause of fatalities in a crisis. In line with the general conception of psychological frailty (see Chapter 1 and 5), this tendency has sometimes been put down to a generalised 'optimistic bias' in human judgement (e.g., Kinsey, Gwynne, Kuligowski, & Kinateder, 2019).

Once again, such accusations rest on the benefit of hindsight. After all, emergency events are exceedingly rare, and if one fled at every sign of possible danger one would waste an awful amount of time and energy. At the time, it is often reasonable to interpret such signs in more mundane terms. Moreover, one is highly dependent upon the interpretation provided by others. Often, the problem lies less with the psychology of the public than with the failure of authorities to identify danger signs and give clear guidance as to how to respond. In the present pandemic, many would argue that fault lies in the hands of those governments which were slow to identify the risks posed by COVID-19 and to introduce appropriate responses, such as physical distancing and lockdown (e.g., Mason, 2020; see also Chapter 18).

A further problem with the notion of 'optimistic bias' is that, in cases where threat becomes more frequent, the notion that 'this can't be happening to us' quickly starts to reverse. For example, in 2017, after a series of terrorist attacks in London, hundreds of people in Oxford Street fled from a noise that turned out to be harmless.

Solidarity is the rule, not the exception

On the whole, the most striking feature of emergencies is the emergence of social support and cooperation. This is true not in every emergency and not for every person in every emergency, but often enough to be mentioned again and again in studies of emergencies and disasters (Solnit, 2009). Importantly, in a disaster, solidarity goes beyond those who are directly affected. Strangers stop to offer help to those they witness in difficulty (Levine & Manning, 2013). People tend to 'converge' on the location of disasters – some simply to look, but many to help, even if they do not have specialist skills. Indeed, more lives are saved by the 'average' citizen, whether 'bystander' or fellow survivor, than by professionals (Helsloot & Ruitenberg, 2004).

Solidarity also outlasts the emergency itself. Many emergencies and disasters involve inequality and injustice – the disaster itself is often a result of inequality, and those already disadvantaged suffer disproportionately (United Nations Office for Disaster Risk Reduction, 2015; see Chapter 17). Accordingly, survivors and bereaved often seek redress, and the 'disaster communities' that arise in the immediate aftermath of crises can evolve to try to meet people's needs for justice. This has been observed after disasters as diverse as the 1985 Mexico City earthquake (Solnit, 2009), the 2011 Fukushima nuclear disaster in Japan (Aldrich, 2013) and the 2017 Grenfell fire in London (Charles, 2019; Tekin Guven & Drury, 2020). As the *Grenfell United* campaign shows, such justice campaigns create yet further solidarities, receiving support from other campaigns and broadening their remit to address other injustices (Renwick, 2019).

The story of COVID-19 is much like the story of disasters in general. Certainly, one can find examples of selfishness: people stockpiling scarce resources like toilet paper, profiteering from hand sanitiser, or ignoring lockdown to drink with their friends. But the frequency of such behaviour was greatly exaggerated by a media which loves nothing more than a story of transgression (D'Urso, 2020; Reicher, Drury, & Stott, 2020a).

However, as indicated in Chapter 1, the real headline of the pandemic – at least in its first phases – has been the extent of adherence to unprecedented restrictions, notably lockdown (e.g., Office for National Statistics, 2020). This in itself is an indication of solidarity, because most people stayed at home less to protect their own health than to minimise the risk of spreading the disease and harming those who were vulnerable (Jackson et al., 2020).

Additionally, virtually everyone has been involved in some informal act of solidarity, knocking on a neighbour's door to see whether they need anything, helping with shopping, setting up WhatsApp groups for one's street, or simply being friendly to others (Monbiot, 2020; see also Chapter 7). There has also been a remarkable flowering of more formal forms of solidarity. In the UK alone, some 1 million people volunteered to help the NHS and over 4,000 mutual aid groups have been formed, involving over 3 million people. There have been so many offers of solidarity that there has sometimes not been enough for people to do (Butler, 2020).

Solidarity trumps selfishness

As psychologists, when we are asked how people behave in emergencies and disasters, the hope and expectation is often that there is a simple answer reflecting general human nature. The 'panic' narrative persists partly because it satisfies that desire. We have argued in this chapter that things are more complicated than this perspective suggests. People can react selfishly, but, as we have shown here, they often respond with solidarity. We have seen this in the wake of COVID-19. Most importantly, though, as psychologists, our aim is not to speculate about how people will act; rather, we seek to identify the factors and understand the processes that determine whether selfishness will trump solidarity, or vice versa. In this way, we are more able to shape what will happen. So, what are these processes? That is the subject of the next chapter.

14

Solidarity

Evangelos Ntontis and
Carolina Rocha

Pandemics inspire the most remarkable acts of unity and compassion (Solnit, 2009). They also lead to appalling acts of division and brutality (Cohn, 2018). The question for this chapter is why and when we come together, rather than fall apart, in crises such as the COVID-19 pandemic. As with all human behaviour, multiple processes at multiple levels are involved. Some involve individual characteristics, such as personal sensitivity towards justice and individual orientations towards prosocial values, or demographic characteristics, such as gender, age and income, all of which have been found to be associated with the likelihood of people exhibiting prosocial behaviours (e.g., Zagefka & James, 2015).

However, the problem with trying to explain behaviour in terms of relatively stable individual differences is that these cannot explain the rapid surge of solidarity (and sometimes, hatred) in a crisis. It is here that group-level explanations come into their own. Research shows that people are more prone to help and empathise with individuals who are perceived as members of the same group than those who are perceived as outgroup members. For instance, Levine and colleagues (2005) took fans of Manchester United and emphasised their club allegiance. These fans then witnessed someone falling over and hurting themselves. This person was wearing either a Manchester United shirt, a Liverpool shirt (both red) or a plain red t-shirt. Participants tended to help the first of these – their fellow Manchester United fan – much more often than the other two.

Collective solidarity is rooted in shared social identity

The fans behaved as they did due to the relational shift that occurs when we have a sense of shared identity with others (a point first discussed in Chapter 2). This flows from the core premise of the social identity approach: that the self is not just about 'me' (and what makes me distinctive) but about 'we' (and what makes my group distinctive). At the group level, this means that what happens to other group members literally happens to my (extended) self. Their fate is my fate. Their sorrows are my sorrows. An insult to one is an injury to all. Hence, I help them in the same way that, as an individual, I help myself. In short, whether I show solidarity to others or not turns on whether I share social identity with them (Yzerbyt & Phalet, 2020).

But we have only told half the story of Levine's Manchester United study. A second condition was run, identical to the first in every respect bar one. The difference was that this time, stress was not on participants' specific fan identity (as supporters of Manchester United), but on the fact that they were football fans. Again, Manchester United fans witnessed someone wearing a Manchester United, a Liverpool, or a plain red t-shirt fall down and hurt themselves. However, in this condition, they helped the injured individual wearing *either* the Manchester United or the Liverpool shirt, but not the person in the plain red t-shirt. While they were still just helping ingroup members, here their identity was more inclusive (as football fans rather than fans of a specific football team), so their solidarity was extended to more people. Those who might otherwise have been seen as rivals to oppose became comrades to whom succour was given (a point we return to in Chapter 20).

The critical point here is that group membership is not a given. It is dynamic and subjective. In different situations, we may see ourselves as individuals or as group members; we may adopt different group memberships in which we share identity with more or less people; and we may define the same group (e.g., the nation) more or less inclusively (see Chapter 2). We can now take a further step in our quest to understand why and when people behave selfishly, or else cooperatively, in a crisis. If solidarity depends upon shared identity in a group, and group membership is variably defined, our task becomes one of understanding how these definitions come about when disaster strikes.

Solidarity is a function of history, context and leadership

Our discussion of how groups are defined in a disaster links up with general discussions we have had about the nature of social identity processes throughout the book thus far – notably in Chapter 2 where we discussed the social identity approach, and in Chapter 3 where we discussed leadership. Consistent with those discussions, when it comes to understanding solidarity, we propose three broad determinants of category definitions: history, contemporary context and leadership.

In terms of history, communities that prove to be resilient in the face of disasters are those characterised by strong and dense pre-existing networks, as well as norms of trust and reciprocity. Such networks are related to increased preparedness before disasters (Reininger et al., 2013), greater solidarity during disasters (Aldrich, 2017), and improved recovery after disasters (Aldrich, 2012).

However, community and communal solidarity can also emerge spontaneously in the immediate context of a crisis, and combine to mobilise solidarity and social support. This can be put down to the experience of 'common fate' in the face of mortal danger. To some extent, everyone faces the same problems both during a disaster and in its aftermath (Ntontis, 2018). Survival depends upon everyone pulling together and so the disaster becomes about the group, not the individual (Ntontis, Drury, Amlôt, Rubin, & Williams, 2019). Evidence from a range of different disasters in different countries (Drury et al., 2019) confirms the link between a sense of shared fate and shared social identity, and also between emergent social identity and solidarity.

The third factor that determines shared identity and solidarity, as discussed in Chapter 3, is leadership and the language that leaders use. Within this pandemic, we have seen a broad range of leadership performance from those (such as Jacinda Ardern in New Zealand and Nicola Sturgeon in Scotland) who consistently framed COVID-19 as affecting a broad and inclusive national community. In contrast, others (such as Prime Minister Narendra Modi in India and President Donald Trump in the US) divided the community, and blamed segments of their country for both the disease itself and for their response to it.

However, good leadership is about more than rhetorical inclusion. It is also about implementing the policies that unify people in practice. It involves addressing the huge inequalities that mean that we are *not* all in this together. The destitute, the marginal and the oppressed are far less able to protect themselves from COVID-19, and are consequently getting infected and dying at far higher rates. In more affluent countries, wealthier people are better able to stay at home than poorer people who need to go out and work (Valentino-DeVries, Lu, & Dance, 2020) – that is, if you have a home in the first place. Homeless people cannot self-isolate (see also Chapter 17). Maintaining a sense of common cause, of shared identity and of solidarity at national and international levels is severely compromised unless leaders address these issues.

Group membership and solidarity are fragile and require long-term investment

Just like journalists, who descend on a disaster at its height and then generally ignore what happens in the aftermath, so researchers tend to concentrate on what happens during disasters, not after disasters. But some researchers have taken a longer-term perspective and asked the question 'Does the sense of togetherness and solidarity endure over time?'. This question is critical because often the greatest problems (such as loss of social networks and livelihoods) are those that emerge long after the immediate drama of a fire or a flood (or a pandemic) has ebbed away (Schonfeld & Demaria, 2015). It is in response to these many problems that groups and solidarity are most important – both for practical reasons and also to maintain the mental and physical well-being of the community (as discussed in Section C).

Common fate and leadership are critical in determining solidarity in a disaster, and are equally critical in ensuring the persistence of solidarity in its aftermath. Research on a flood-hit area 18 months after the disaster showed that inequalities in the post-disaster treatment of different groups and the return of pre-disaster group boundaries undermined any sense of common fate (Ntontis, Drury, Amlôt, Rubin, & Williams, 2020; see also Chapter 17). However, this decline is not inevitable. The persistence of secondary stressors (to the extent that they are perceived in collective terms) and of equitable social support can help maintain shared social identity. This can also be actively sustained by regular collective rituals, such as commemorative events (Norris & Kaniasty, 1996).

In summary, we have sought to make two main points in this chapter. First, solidarity in a crisis like COVID-19 is a function of shared social identity. Second, shared social identity is a function of the creation of inclusive social categories, and whether this happens depends on history, contemporary context and leadership. But what should those tasked with responding to crises, and specifically to pandemics and other health crises, actually do? That is what we discuss in Chapter 15.

15

Managing Crowds in Crises

Holly Carter, Dale Weston and Richard Amlôt

In this chapter, we build upon the general theme of the last – that is, the importance and the potential of shared social identity to support the COVID-19 response. However, where previously the emphasis was on unity and solidarity between members of the public (e.g., to explain helping), here we address relations between the public and authorities or leaders (e.g., those seeking to increase compliance with physical distance measures). We argue that the consequences of shared identity, which have been shown to be so important in building an effective community response to the pandemic – the mutual trust, influence and support, are equally important when it comes to community–authority relations.

Shared social identity between authorities and the public is the key to an effective pandemic response

At one level, shared identity is necessary if people are to trust government and hence adhere to the restrictions it puts in place (such as lockdown). At another level, people must be willing to listen to officials, to accept the information they provide, and to cooperate with them (Carter, Drury, & Amlôt, 2018). For instance, the success of contact tracing relies on people's willingness to reveal their contacts if they test positive for COVID-19. However, shared identity between public and authorities is about more than the public obeying instructions from authorities and leaders. Compliance will only ensue when authorities respect and trust the public. Indeed, as we discussed in Chapter 4, it is only when trust is *mutual* that it becomes possible to formulate, internalise and unite around shared norms concerning health protective behaviours (e.g., Carter, Drury, Rubin, Williams, & Amlôt, 2014; Carter, Drury, Amlôt, Rubin, & Williams, 2015; Carter, Drury, Rubin, Williams, & Amlôt, 2015).

Interestingly, these norms are about behaviours that protect the community more than the individual. Hence, if successfully implemented, they create a virtuous cascade of effects. When we see others abide by these norms (e.g., staying home despite the temptation to go out) we grow in trust for others and our sense of shared identity within our communities is strengthened. Moreover, we gain the confidence to challenge those few who violate the norms, secure in the belief that we are acting with the support of others. In this way, communities *self-regulate* rather than needing the police to intervene and enforce regulations (Drury, Novelli, & Stott, 2015).

This means that shared identity between authorities and the public has consequences that mirror, and are every bit as important and consequential for the response to COVID-19, as shared identity among the public itself. However, when we turn from the consequences to the antecedents of shared identity, we begin to see key differences between community–community and community–authority relations. While we showed in Chapter 14 that shared identification between members of the public can arise spontaneously due to a sense of shared fate, the relationship between emergency responders and members of the public is more complex. The authorities and the community are self-evidently *not* in the same boat in a disaster. Those in a fire engine and those in a fire have very different experiences, as do those deciding on lockdown and those *being* locked down in this pandemic. As a consequence, the relationship between authorities and the public can never be taken for granted. It must always be worked on and actively nurtured – a central element in that work has to do with what is referred to as *procedural justice* (Tyler, 2006).

If authorities treat us with fairness, if their encounters with us display trust and respect, and if they listen to us and explain to us how lockdown restrictions are in our interests, then they convey to us that, rather than being an alien force imposed upon us, we are jointly bound together in partnership. In other words, procedural justice promotes shared identity, and therefore all the positive effects described above (Carter, Drury, Amlôt, et al., 2015). Moreover, as our description suggests, one cannot create a sense of procedural justice and hence of partnership without effective communication (e.g., Carter et al., 2018). Accordingly, in what follows, we suggest five general principles for interacting with the public during major incidents and disasters in order to create shared identity and ensure trust and adherence. These principles can also be used to evaluate the performance of authorities in crises, such as presented by the COVID-19 pandemic.

Research supports five key principles for interacting with the public in a crisis

1. Understand that the way in which responders perceive and manage an incident will affect the way in which members of the public behave – and plan accordingly

Guidance and training for responders and authorities often describe public behaviour during mass emergencies in terms of the 'panic' perspective outlined in Chapter 13 (Carter & Amlôt, 2016). This can lead responders to view the public with hostility, which alienates them, undermines compliance, and produces the very behaviours one is seeking to avoid (Carter et al., 2014, 2018). However, as we noted, behaviour in emergencies is often orderly, cooperative and constructive. This leads to a very different approach, which seeks to support and 'scaffold' activity rather than to control the public. It is essential that authorities understand this and plan accordingly, consulting with behavioural science and communication experts throughout the incident.

Accordingly, the key question to be asked of the COVID-19 response is whether, when the number of infections were dramatically increasing, the authorities treated the population as a problem, prone to panic and needing to be controlled. Alternatively, did they treat members of the public as partners, acknowledging, supporting and harnessing the multiple forms of mutual aid which developed in local communities? In short, did the authorities trust the people?

2. Communicate openly and honestly about the nature of an incident, explaining why certain actions are (or are not) being taken

It is vital that authorities communicate openly and honestly with members of the public about what actions they are taking to manage an incident, and why they are taking those actions (Carter et al., 2018). Openness is another key dimension of procedural justice and of building shared identity between responders and the public that encourages adherence (Carter, Drury, Rubin, Williams, & Amlôt, 2015). Conversely, being seen to withhold information (which can result from a fear that people will panic if told about the dangers they face) can destroy any sense of togetherness and create suspicion between responders and the public.

Were the authorities open with the public? Did they explain the measures they took to control the spread of COVID-19 in the community and make available the scientific advice that lay behind them? If we look at the UK, the government has taken the unprecedented steps of naming their advisory committees and allowing access to some of the papers that describe scientific advice they have received (UK Government, 2020). This has won them support, but for some people it has not gone far enough (*The Guardian*, 2020).

3. Communicate in a timely way

The way in which the first minutes, hours or days an incident are managed will be crucial for shaping the subsequent nature of the relationship between authorities and members of the public. Authorities should therefore begin communicating immediately and should not wait until all information is known before initiating communication. Where information is not yet available, this should be explained, and updates should be provided as soon as further information becomes available. Regular updates should be provided, even if no new information is known. In all these ways, trust is created and maintained. As we saw from Chapter 13, timely information about dangers – and hence timely reaction – is critical to avoid fatalities.

Did the authorities communicate and respond to the dangers of COVID-19 early enough? In a number of countries, the issue of whether governments reacted too slowly has been a subject of heated debate. For example, despite officials' fears that conditions would be conducive to COVID-19's spread, thousands of Valencia soccer supporters were allowed to travel to Milan in February 2020 to watch their team play in the Champions League. It is highly likely that, after having been in the stadium with 40,000 fans from the Italian city Bergamo (a city at the epicentre of Italy's COVID-19 outbreak), the virus travelled home to Spain with the Valencia fans. This at least partly explains the high infection rate in Valencia in subsequent weeks (Hawley, 2020).

4. Explain how taking recommended protective actions will promote public health

Advice in an emergency must always be concise and precise so that people know exactly what behaviours are required of them (Michie, Van Stralen, & West, 2011). But it is not enough to tell people what to do (indeed that can provoke resistance). It is also essential to take people into one's trust and explain to them why these behaviours are necessary and in their own interests – or, to be more exact, why they are in the interests of their community (see Chapter 14). Accordingly, to bring people on board in a pandemic it is important to provide health-focused information which explains how desired actions will reduce risks to health so that their loved ones and other members of their community are protected. Conversely, it is necessary to explain how proscribed actions will increase risks to loved ones and community members (Carter, Drury, Amlôt, et al., 2015; Carter, Drury, Rubin, et al., 2015, 2018).

In the COVID-19 context, was messaging on protective measures sufficiently clear, and did it explain the basis for these measures? In Britain, many have argued that the earlier advice 'Stay Home, Protect the NHS, Save Lives' was clear about what was required and clear about the reasons why: to 'flatten the curve' of infection and ensure that the health service was not overwhelmed. Indeed, in a poll of 6,500 people, 91% reported that they felt the slogan made it clear what they had to do (Smith, 2020a). By contrast, an updated slogan, 'Stay Alert, Control the Virus, Save Lives', unveiled as lockdown measures began to be lifted, saw only 30% of respondents in the same survey reporting that they were clear about what they were meant to do.

5. Ensure that members of the public are able to undertake recommended actions

Motivation may be important, but it is not sufficient to get people to act on advice. People must also have the opportunity to do what is asked of them (Michie et al., 2011). Telling people to physically distance at work when they are employed in sites where distancing is impossible, or to avoid crowding in public transport when they have no other means of travel, is likely only to create resentment. This means that authorities must identify potential barriers to adherence and empower people to overcome them – through enhanced communication, increased physical support, financial measures and so on (Bonell et al., 2020; see also Chapter 17).

How such questions are dealt with in different countries is central to whether the authorities are seen as guardians or as oppressors in the fight against COVID-19. Indeed, it is central to whether societies work together to contain the virus or turn on each other. This is an issue we unpack further in the section's next and final chapter.

16

Social Order and Disorder

Clifford Stott and Matt Radburn

So far, the chapters in this section have concentrated primarily on the positive side of collective behaviour: solidarity with others in the community, and identification with and adherence to authority. A sense that 'we are all in this together' has led people in many countries to accept – even to embrace – a level of surveillance and restriction on personal freedom that might ordinarily lead to fury (see also Chapter 4). However, acceptance has not been universal. For example, in early April 2020 in Mumbai, migrant workers fought with police outside Bandra railway station during a protest against a COVID-19 lockdown (Kaonga, 2020). In Chile, conflict developed in protests against lockdown-induced food shortages for the poor (Fuentes, 2020). So when and why does such disorder arise, and how can governments and police forces act to prevent it?

Understanding disorder requires an understanding of collective history and culture

Our first point should be self-evident by now: disorder is not inevitable, even in hard times, or when people are deprived of the things that they normally take for granted (such as the right to go out for a walk). Nor is disorder a 'natural' consequence of collective psychology. What we see in this pandemic is what we always see: crowds are rarely violent. As we touched on in Chapter 12, when violence does occur, we need to look to the interaction between collective conceptions of rights and the nature of government interventions: where the former is seen to be trampled by the latter, trouble ensues.

Studies show that state interventions to control outbreaks of disease can violate collective conceptions of rights by being too harsh or poorly targeted (Harrison, 2012). They can also do so by being weak, tardy or just plain absent, in ways that indicate a lack of concern for whether people live or die. Indeed, a CIA analysis claims that the inability of some nations to provide adequate health care for their population has fuelled insurgencies against them (CIA, 2000).

Looking closer, the specific interventions that provoke conflict are those which display insensitivity to specific collective beliefs and cultural norms – often those surrounding death. In the 1890s, riots occurred in Egypt and Tashkent due to interference in Muslim burial rites (Sahadeo, 2005). During a cholera epidemic in Italy 1910, restrictions on traditional modes of burial sparked attacks on health workers, police and hospitals (Snowden, 1995).

Looking closer still, another factor emerges. In these various cases, it was not simply that cherished customs were restricted, it was that state intervention was selectively applied. The poor were targeted, while powerful elites found ways to circumvent restrictions. When conflict occurs, the issue of fairness is never far away. And if conflict occurs in a particular site (say around burial practices), it is generally because this can be harnessed to highlight a range of underlying inequities and grievances (see Chapter 2).

Taken together, the historical evidence suggests that social disorder arises through the relationship between social structural inequalities, collective beliefs and forms of state intervention. The lesson for today, as nation states struggle to curtail the spread of COVID-19, is that any intervention needs to be carefully planned in acknowledgement of underlying structural issues, so that these issues are attenuated rather than exacerbated. What then are the implications of this for what governments and police should actually do?

Effective policing requires dialogue, respect, trust and neutrality

The previous chapter introduced the concept of procedural justice as a central element in obedience to authority (Tyler, 2006). The central issue was whether people will listen to their authorities and responders. In this chapter, we are primarily interested in how people respond to the police. Here, procedural justice is, if anything, even more critical (Maguire, Khade, & Mora, 2020) – especially the core proposition that people comply less through fear of punishment ('instrumental compliance') than because they are convinced that what they are being asked to do is the right thing to do ('normative compliance'; Turner, 1991;

see Chapter 4). In short, the most effective tool the police can have is *legitimacy*: the sense that they are doing the right thing for us.

Meares (2013) has translated this idea into four general rules that the police should observe in all their dealings with the public. The first is that in their encounters with police officers, people value having an opportunity to have '*voice*' – that is, to put across their own view. The second is that people expect police officers to treat them with *dignity and respect*. The third principle is *trust*: people want the police to display benevolence and be well-intentioned. The fourth is that people value police *neutrality*: they want police officers to make their decisions based on the 'facts' of the situation rather than on the basis of prejudices or personal 'biases'.

More concretely, during the COVID-19 pandemic the general principles of procedural justice and Meares' four rules have been translated into the 'Four 'Es' guidance issued by the UK College of Policing to all UK local police forces (College of Policing, 2020). This advises police officers that their starting point should be to 'Engage' with the public. Then, rather than simply issuing instructions, they should 'Explain' what they want people to do and why. The next step is to 'Encourage' people to comply. Only if these dialogue-based approaches have been thoroughly tried and have failed should officers even consider turning to the more coercive fourth E: 'Enforce.'

But on what basis should the police explain their actions and hence encourage (or ultimately enforce) compliance? The College of Policing document is explicit on this matter. It recommends that people are asked to observe restrictions in order to protect the National Health Service and save lives. In other words, the police are to explain that they are acting to protect the health of the public. In this way, policing takes us beyond Meares' rules and the notion of procedural justice as simply about fairness in the abstract and the process of interaction. Rather, the key thing is to persuade the people that the police are *serving the public interest* (Reicher & Stott, 2020).

Taking this argument a step further, the important thing is that the effectiveness of the police depends upon being seen *by* the community as being *of* the community and acting *for* the community (Radburn & Stott, 2019), both in their style of interaction with the public and in the substantive content of what they do and say. It is this combination of being seen as both 'of' and 'for' a community that is critical. One cannot persuasively claim to be acting in the interests of the community while treating community members in a way that one would not treat 'us'. Equally, one will gain little credibility by treating community members as 'us' if most of one's actions go against community interests (Trinkner, Jackson, & Tyler, 2018).

Ineffective policing ignores and exacerbates social inequalities

If policing by consent derives from the police being seen as 'of us and for us', the corollary is that dissent arises when the police are seen as 'not of us and against us'. The potential for this is ever-present in deeply divided societies, especially given that the pandemic, far from being a great leveller, exacerbates those divides (see Chapters 17 and 18). As has been stressed throughout this book, lockdown is a very different experience for those whose lives are more or less precarious. The same restrictions on going out have a very unequal impact on people who live in crowded flats or spacious houses with gardens. Whether or not the police treat you with respect and with understanding of your situation when outdoors can make all the difference in terms of whether or not the incipient divide comes out into the open.

As Tyler has argued, every encounter between a police officer and a member of the public is a teachable moment in which whole communities 'learn about the law and legal authorities' (Tyler, 2012, p. 12). But this moment is not divorced from the wider experience of these communities. If it aligns with the sense that 'we are all in this together', then it can contribute to the preservation of order. If, however, it aligns with the sense that 'my group gets a raw deal', then it can be the beginnings of social disorder. In short, whether at the theoretical level or at the level of the participants' experience, it is critical to relate what goes on in an encounter between the police and a member of the public (especially minority group members) to social structural realities and the formation of social identities (Stott & Radburn, 2020).

Moreover, every encounter matters because it does not just affect those directly involved. A whole community can draw lessons from a single incident. As discussed in Chapter 12, an insult to one group member can be experienced as an injury by all and evoke anger in all. Characteristically, riots start from an iconic event that is seen to encapsulate the various inequalities, indignities and oppressions suffered by the group: the shooting of Michael Brown in Ferguson (Lowery, 2016) or of Michael Duggan in Tottenham (Reicher & Stott, 2011). Moreover, riots often occur in waves. As the first incident hits the headlines, it serves to emphasise collective antagonisms and grievances. Divides that may not previously have been at the forefront of consciousness can no longer be ignored. But it is not just that a riot can lead members of a common group in different locations to feel a common resentment towards the police; also, they often feel more empowered to act, having seen their peers take on the police (Stott et al., 2018).

The lessons here for the current COVID-19 crisis are clear – that there is a real risk of sustained social disorder if the policing of the pandemic is insensitive to the structural inequalities that divide us. This is a point that will be explored further in the next chapter.

Beware of complacency

In many ways, this chapter serves as a warning against complacency. In this book we have emphasised and celebrated the many positives of group psychology. But even in those societies which have been most successful in creating an inclusive sense of shared social identity, that accomplishment is fragile. There remain deep divisions in all our societies. The potential for those divisions to open up and shatter our hard-won unity against COVID-19 is always there. The way the pandemic is policed is critical to that potential and determines whether it becomes a reality, for the way we encounter 'the state' is generally through our encounters with the police. The way we are treated by the police tells us where we stand in society. If this treatment confirms the broader injustices to which our group has been subjected, then everything falls apart.

SECTION E

INTERGROUP RELATIONS

Hopefully, one day soon we will live in a world where COVID-19 does not dominate every aspect of our lives. It is nonetheless clear that when this day comes, the world will have been changed dramatically. To understand these changes, we need to explore the role of collective processes in determining both how the COVID-19 story unfolds, and the ways the virus is contained and responded to. Viruses do not discriminate, but just about every other aspect of society does. Everything from a person's capacity to avoid infection to their likelihood of avoiding financial hardship is determined by group-level status and power inequalities, many of which are determined by pre-COVID-19 intergroup relations. It is an understanding of these power and status dynamics at the collective level that will help us understand the long-term impact of this pandemic on society and, by extension, the individuals in it. This knowledge is also necessary for us to work collectively to craft the best possible future.

In this final section of the book, we focus first on the effect of pre-existing group-based *inequality* on the COVID-19 response – inequality between the poor and the wealthy, between minorities and majorities, and between the disadvantaged and advantaged (Chapter 17). We also consider how COVID-19 is likely to shape those relationships. We then outline how *polarisation* along ideological lines determines the way that groups respond to the immediate challenges that the COVID crisis poses, and how the crisis will impact political rifts (Chapter 18). After this, we explore how COVID-19 has coloured (and will continue to colour) our perceptions of specific groups in society (e.g., Asians), triggering new forms of intergroup hostility and exacerbating and legitimising some old forms of *prejudice and racism* (Chapter 19). Clearly, solidarity and a sense of shared identity will be crucial for holding communities together as we seek to cope with the long-term societal consequences of the virus. We draw the book to a close with a discussion of how this might be achieved through the cultivation of a *common identity* (Chapter 20).

17

Inequality

Jolanda Jetten

Social distancing is a privilege. It means you live in a house large
enough to practice it. Hand washing is a privilege too. It means you
have access to running water. Hand sanitisers are a privilege. It means
you have money to buy them. Lockdowns are a privilege. It means you
can afford to be at home. Most of the ways to ward the Corona off are
accessible only to the affluent. In essence, a disease that was spread by
the rich as they flew around the globe will now kill millions of the poor.
(Anonymous Indian doctor, cited by Tomazin, 2020)

The poor and the stigmatised in society are more vulnerable to disasters than
the affluent and privileged. This is not a new observation. For example, in the
aftermath of Hurricane Katrina in New Orleans, it became clear that poor and
black residents were disproportionately affected by the floodwaters. The sociol-
ogist Erikson captured this well, observing 'The portion of the New Orleans
population that lives below sea level and the portion that lived below the poverty line turned out to be largely the same' (Erikson, 1976/2006, Prologue).
Accordingly, as the opening quote to this chapter suggests, when it comes to
understanding whose health and financial situation has been most negatively
affected by COVID-19, we need to focus on the disadvantaged in society, not
the advantaged.

COVID-19 targets and exacerbates group-based disadvantage

One powerful explanation of the unequal impact of the virus relates to the *resources* available to the 'haves' and the 'have-nots'. For example, those on lower wages are less likely to engage in physical distancing, for the simple reason that they are unlikely to be able to work from home and unable to avoid crowded public transport when getting to work (Ogbunu, 2020). Indeed, location data from 15 million US phone users revealed that limiting movement was a luxury that low-income people were less likely to be able to afford. While everyone moved around less once physical distancing measures were introduced, wealthier people were more likely to stay at home sooner and more often. This effect was most pronounced during the work week, which suggests that this difference was due primarily to the fact that people with higher incomes tended to have greater flexibility to work from home. More affluent people had a physical distancing 'head start', reducing their exposure to the virus at a crucial point in time and hence diminishing their risk of falling ill (Valentino-DeVries et al., 2020).

Moreover, low-income employees are less likely to be in secure employment than their high-income counterparts, and less likely to benefit from protective equipment and measures that allow them to do their work safely (Scheiber & Conger, 2020). Even if a person's job can hypothetically be done remotely, in order to work effectively from home one needs to have high-speed internet and an appropriate office space. Again, this is more likely to be true the more affluent one is (Reeves & Rothwell, 2020). At the household level, a person's wealth determines the extent to which they can stockpile food and other necessities, and therefore the frequency with which they need to leave their houses and be exposed to the virus (Reeves & Rothwell, 2020).

In summary, like any disaster, COVID-19 has hit the most vulnerable the hardest. As Erikson (1976/2006) notes, simple geography partly explains why the vulnerable end up bearing the brunt of natural or human-made disasters:

> Tsunamis do not seek out the poor; the poor are shoved out to those low-lying areas where the land meets the sea. Earthquakes do not seek out the ill-housed; they strike evenly at all of the structures in their way, but do the most damage to the frailest and most shoddily built of them, the ones in which the needy have been invited to live. Toxic waters do not seek out the least protected; they are deposited on the same parcels of land where the poorly protected, in their turn, have been deposited. (Erikson, 1976/2006, Prologue)

While this is true, it is important to add that those who are vulnerable do not 'find themselves' in those vulnerable places by accident. Indeed, the poor have not been 'deposited' on dangerous dumping grounds through sheer bad luck. In order to understand what put and kept them there, we need to understand the dynamics of intergroup power and status that legitimise and consolidate their disadvantage (Tajfel & Turner, 1979). As Ashwin Vasan, a public health professor at Columbia University, observed about COVID-19, 'People want to talk about this virus as an equal opportunity pathogen, but it's really not. . . . It's going right to the fissures in our society' (cited in Valentino-DeVries et al., 2020).

In short, the harm caused by COVID-19 differs as a function of status and power inequalities in any given society. The more division there is, the more harm it does.

Group-level disadvantage compromises health and hence resistance to COVID-19

While economic inequality limits the ability of those at the bottom of a status hierarchy to materially protect themselves against COVID-19, there is another reason why it is the poor, the stigmatised and minorities who are most vulnerable to the virus. This relates to the oft-observed social gradient in health whereby people are more likely to be healthy and less likely to have underlying health conditions if they are more affluent, white, and living in a Western country (Haslam, Jetten et al., 2018; Marmot, 2015). In the context of COVID-19, this means, for example, that because pre-existing health conditions such as diabetes, respiratory conditions and heart disease are more prevalent in disadvantaged groups, it is more likely that members of those groups will be harmed (and killed) by the virus (Reeves & Rothwell, 2020).

Why do the disadvantaged have chronically poorer health than the advantaged? There are a number of reasons, the most obvious being that poverty reduces people's access to relevant resources (including treatment and advice; see Haslam, Jetten et al., 2018, for a detailed discussion). From a social identity perspective, what is particularly relevant is that disadvantage typically goes hand in hand with being the target of stigma (Jetten et al., 2017). This means that the negative effects of disadvantage on health are partly grounded in group-based discrimination and exclusion on the basis of group membership (Paradies et al., 2015; Schmitt, Branscombe, Postmes, & Garcia, 2014). Because of this, we expect that membership of stigmatised groups (e.g., those centring on ethnicity and social class) will have its own independent negative impact on people's ability to cope with COVID-19. For example, it is clear that in the US a combination of poverty, discrimination and low-quality care serves to create 'a perfect storm' for African-Americans following COVID-19 infection. In the state of Louisiana this has meant that while African-Americans constitute just a third of the general population, they have suffered more than 70% of COVID-related deaths (ABC News, 2020).

Inequality will almost certainly increase in the aftermath of the COVID-19 crisis

It is not just that infection rates differ for the haves and the have-nots. The longer-term economic consequences of COVID-19 will also vary widely for those in different socio-economic groups. As Torsten Bell of the Resolution Foundation noted, 'the virus doesn't discriminate between people but the accompanying economic shock certainly does' (*The Economist*, 2020).

There is good evidence that, in the aftermath of most disasters, inequality (i.e., the gap between the poorest and the wealthiest in society; Jetten et al., 2017) increases and deepens. For example, research showed that in the years following the disastrous flooding of the Brisbane River in 2011, the difference in annual income between those on low and middle incomes increased by AU$7,000 a year (Ulubasoglu, 2020). The reasons for this intensification of inequality are complex; one is that lower income workers are most likely to be temporarily unemployed because of a disaster (e.g., in the case of COVID-19, those in the tourism and hospitality industry), and are not able to easily make up for the income lost over this time. Furthermore, employees on casual contracts and with little job security are more likely to be without income for a considerable period. Lower income earners are also less likely to be insured for disasters and, consistent with Erikson's (1976/2006) reasoning, are more likely to live in hazard-prone areas. This means that they are not only more likely to be harder hit by a disaster, but also that it is more likely that they have limited means to recover from such disasters. In contrast, those on full-time contracts and with higher incomes typically less affected. Indeed, sometimes they may even benefit financially from a disaster (e.g., because lobbying enhances the likelihood that financial support systems will be developed with them in mind; Beaini & Ulubasoglu, 2019).

Group-based inequality undermines social solidarity

The foregoing discussion suggests that economic dynamics are often a key cause of deepened income inequality following disasters. In the case of COVID-19, for example, it seems likely that the businesses and communities that benefit most from financial recovery packages will be those that are most prosperous (Kristof, 2020; Ulubasoglu, 2020). Importantly, these dynamics are also partly psychological; social identity theorising suggests that they will often be grounded in collective-level processes and intergroup relations. This is because some of the key defining features of communities and countries experiencing high levels of economic inequality are low in cohesiveness and characterised by strong 'us-versus-them' dynamics (Jetten et al., 2017; Jetten & Peters, 2019; see also Chapter 18). Furthermore, with high inequality comes low trust and high competitiveness – both ingredients that undermine a coordinated response to a disaster.

As we saw in Section C, whether a community bands together or falls apart in the face of a disaster depends very much on whether people have a strong sense of shared identity before the disaster (Muldoon et al., 2019). In the context of a contagious virus where the actions of others determine whether infection spreads or not, issues of trust and solidarity are likely to be especially important (Rao & Greve Insead, 2018). Given its capacity to undermine trust, pre-existing inequality will be one of the key determinants of whether chaos or solidarity prevails in the wake of disaster.

Practically speaking, does this mean that communities and societies with high levels of inequality are doomed and that, by definition, they will be more harmed by COVID-19 both in the immediate and the longer term? No. High inequality does not determine outcomes, but is instead an *obstacle* in the path to recovery. Accordingly, even though inequality is often deeply embedded in societal structures and therefore not easily reduced, it is instructive to consider ways in which its negative effects on solidarity, trust and community cohesion can be countered. The lessons of previous sections on how *building shared social identity* can enhance effective leadership, social connectedness and solidarity in the face of the pandemic are critical when developing policy around these issues.

This recommendation to focus on building group-based ties sits well with the conclusions of Rao and Greve Insead (2018). In their analysis of community resilience in the aftermath of the Spanish flu, they conclude that, because contagious diseases undermine cooperation in society, rebuilding needs to focus on boosting community cooperation and identification:

> The typical response to pandemics includes isolation and treatment, home quarantines, closure of schools, cancellation of large-scale public meetings, and other steps to reduce social density. While these immediate responses are entirely practical, policy planners should also consider how a pandemic impairs the social infrastructure of a community over

the long term, and undertake initiatives to foster the building of community organizations. After all, if it is sociable communities that survive disasters by helping themselves, investments in enhancing the social infrastructure of communities too merit consideration. (Rao & Greve Insead, 2018, p. 21)

We could not agree more.

18

Polarisation

Charlie R. Crimston and Hema Preya Selvanathan

This virus is dangerous. It exploits cracks between us. . . . Take as an example, ideology, or in one country it could be the differences along party lines. It exploits that. That's why I said we need national unity and whoever has whatever ideology – whether that person is from left or right or centre – they should work together to fight this virus to save these real people. If we don't do that, this virus will stay longer with us to kill more people and we will lose more precious lives. (Dr Tedros Adhanom Ghebreyesus, Director-General of the World Health Organization; World Health Organization, 2020)

On the surface, a pandemic is not an ideological issue. However, in many parts of the world, political ideology was key to how individuals and nations viewed, discussed and responded to COVID-19. There are at least two ways in which political division and polarisation might shape our individual and collective responses to the COVID-19 crisis. First, partisan differences might slow a society's response to COVID-19. Second, perceived political polarisation can contribute to a breakdown in the fabric of society. This may shape not only individual protective behaviours, but also the nature of post-COVID-19 society. We will unpack these two points in turn.

Partisan differences create us-versus-them dynamics which undermine effective responses to disaster

As COVID-19 began to spread across the globe, political ideology and partisan splits influenced the way that many world leaders responded to the crisis, and the extent to which ordinary citizens viewed the virus as a real and present threat. For example, at a political rally in February, US President Donald Trump declared: 'The Democrats are politicizing the coronavirus. You know that, right? Coronavirus. They're politicizing it' (Bump, 2020). In Brazil, although Health Minister Luiz Henrique Mandetta called for people to follow social isolation guidelines, President Jair Bolsonaro downplayed the threat of the virus and threatened to fire members of his cabinet who dissented (leading two of his health ministers to resign; Sandy & Milhorance, 2020).

As the pandemic unfolded, the fact that leaders in some countries blamed political rivals for using alarmist language served to accentuate pre-existing 'us-versus-them' dynamics. This was perhaps most obvious in the US, where political polarisation was already on the rise, and where the looming presidential election was a focus for divergent party interests (Schaeffer, 2020). As a result, a threat that was initially not political became political.

The dynamic can be understood in terms of the *fit principle* articulated within self-categorization theory (Oakes et al., 1994; see Chapter 2). More specifically, framing the threat of COVID-19 as an 'us-versus-them' issue increased the likelihood that people would perceive the virus through the lens of their political affiliation. In the US, Democrats and Republicans thus came to view the threat very differently as they converged on attitudes and beliefs that were (seen to be) consistent with divergent ingroup norms. In particular, Democrats prioritised health and well-being, whereas Republicans prioritised individual freedom and economic growth. Among other things, this meant that Democrats were more concerned about the virus (Butchireddygari, 2020). For example, data collected by the Pew Research Center in March indicated that while 59% of Democrat voters viewed COVID-19 as a major threat to the US population, the same was true for only 33% of Republicans (Scanlan, 2020).

Such polarisation is consequential because it fuels intergroup tensions and conflict; in countries like the US, an issue that arguably should not have been viewed through an ideological lens came to divide people along political lines – precisely at a time when they desperately needed a coordinated and cohesive response to the pandemic. Problems were compounded by the fact that partisan perceptions of the virus also affected people's health-related behaviour.

In the US, this is demonstrated by smartphone location data which showed that people in Republican-dominated regions were much less likely to practise physical distancing than those in Democrat regions, even after controlling for state policies, population density and local COVID-19 cases and deaths (Allcott et al., 2020).

In these different ways, it is apparent that polarisation and partisan bickering contributed to a slowed response to COVID-19 in countries like the US (Van Bavel, 2020). As well as leading some people not to take adequate precautions, this also led others to campaign actively against preventative measures (e.g., in demonstrations to end the lockdown). These campaigns not only took a toll on social cohesion but also cost lives.

Polarisation promotes the breakdown of social fabric

While partisan differences no doubt slowed COVID-19 responses in a number of countries, the actual levels of polarisation in society are only half the story. The extent to which people *perceive* there to be polarisation in their society is also important. Indeed, there is evidence that the perceived level of polarisation is a stronger predictor of negative outcomes than actual polarisation (Enders & Armaly, 2019). More specifically, higher perceived polarisation in society has been linked to reduced intergroup trust, efficacy and altruism, as well as to increased outgroup hostility, selfishness and competition (Arvan, 2019; Enders & Armaly, 2019). This negative impact on societal trust is robust across cultures (Rapp, 2016) and seems to increase in times of uncertainty (Sherman, Hogg, & Maitner, 2009).

In times of crisis, the effects of polarisation can create a tipping point for societies whose cohesion is chronically damaged. If people perceive their society to be polarised, they are more likely to think that it is breaking down (i.e., so that they are in a state of *anomie*; Crimston, Selvanathan, & Jetten, 2020). Social identity theorising suggests that this in turn will mean that they are less likely to trust either their leaders or their fellow citizens to do the right thing. So at a time when what is really needed is social solidarity, one is likely instead to see a society where 'everyone is out for themselves' (see also Section D).

We tested this prediction in the context of COVID-19. In line with the social identity analysis outlined above, we expected that higher perceived polarisation might lead individuals to engage in *personally* self-protective behaviours – that is, behaviours intended to minimise their own risk of being infected with the virus (e.g., avoiding crowds and public spaces, washing hands more frequently;

see Figure 7). At the end of March 2020, we surveyed 1,000 adults across the US and the UK to gauge their sense of the level of political polarisation in their society and their attitudes towards the COVID-19 crisis. We found that people who perceived political polarisation within their country over the past 10 years were more likely to believe that their government had responded in a chaotic and disorganised manner to the COVID-19 crisis. In other words, perceived polarisation predicted a sense of COVID-related anomie. As predicted, this anomie was associated with an increase in personally self-protective behaviour. Essentially, people who recalled a history of political division in their society were more likely to see a society in chaos during the pandemic, and to believe that in order to survive this pandemic, they needed to assume an individualistic stance in which they took responsibility for protection from the virus into their own hands.

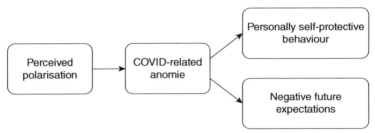

Figure 7   The effects of perceived polarisation

Engaging in more personally self-protective behaviours in the face of COVID-19 may have been a good thing in so far as it served to reduce the spread of the virus. However, perceived political polarisation and anomie are likely to have other more negative long-term consequences. If people feel that their country has been politically divided, this does not bode well for their collective future (Liu & Hilton, 2005). Consistent with this supposition, we found that our respondents' perceptions of political polarisation prior to COVID-19 were indirectly associated with them having more negative expectations about the post-COVID-19 future. As with self-protective behaviours, this was driven by a heightened sense of anomie. More specifically, respondents' negative expectations included doubts about the future vitality of their country and its economy, and increased pessimism about the future of humanity as a whole. So not only does seeing one's country as politically divided in the past make you feel that society is breaking down in the present, but it also makes you concerned that chaos will continue to reign in the future.

Political polarisation can be overcome by building a strong sense of 'us'

The foregoing analysis suggests that COVID-19 represents not only a health crisis, but also a political one – at least in those societies where it serves to accentuate pre-existing divisions. What, then, can societies do to overcome political polarisation? While political division and polarisation are not new, in order to overcome a crisis of this scale it is essential for groups to unite at a superordinate level. As discussed in Section B, when making crucial decisions, leaders need to fix their eyes firmly on the well-being of their citizens, not their own political survival. Saving lives depends on political leaders and authorities taking quick and coordinated action, but this is only possible if partisan differences are put to one side (a conclusion also endorsed by *The Lancet*, 2020). As we saw in Chapter 3, this means that leaders need to engage in effective identity leadership by emphasising that they speak for, and act on behalf of, *all* citizens regardless of their political loyalties (see also Chapters 7 and 20).

Fortunately, in the context of the COVID-19 crisis, there were many instances of effective identity leadership that were not hampered by ideological squabbles or fractured politics. For example, Singapore has long been ruled by a single political party that maintains tight control over citizens and mass media (Barron, 2020). This fact (and the associated absence of partisan divisions) appears to have helped Prime Minister Lee Hsien Loong to immediately set in motion a coordinated and effective government response (albeit one whose focus on the Singaporean ingroup neglected the circumstances of migrant workers, whose poor living conditions later became a site for major outbreaks of infection; Yea, 2020).

However, effective responses to COVID-19 have not been confined to authoritarian and one-party states. There have also been clear demonstrations of bipartisan unity in strong democracies with multiple major political parties. This was seen when the Dutch Prime Minister, Mark Rutte, appointed the opposition health minister to join the government, after the sitting health minister collapsed from exhaustion and later resigned (Holroyd, 2020). It was also seen in South Africa, where all 14 political parliamentary parties worked together to develop measures aimed at mitigating the spread of the virus. According to President Cyril Ramaphosa, they 'agreed that regardless of our political persuasions, our political differences, all of us share a common desire to keep our people safe' (Powell, 2020). Likewise, New Zealand's Prime Minister, Jacinda Ardern, reacted quickly to curb the spread of the virus, repeatedly calling for cross-party unity to defeat COVID-19 (Duncan, 2020). This call for unity was reflected in the words of her primary political opponent, the leader of New Zealand's National Party:

Today we could look backward at what's been done well and perhaps not so well. It is not a time for that. We are where we are and we are all in this together. And today on the big questions, in this House and in New Zealand we agree, there's no National or Labour, or Green or ACT or New Zealand First, just New Zealanders. (Bridges, 2020)

This is a model that other nations would have been wise to follow. Certainly, we imagine it is the preferred model for the many thousands of New Zealanders who might otherwise have lost their lives in the pandemic.

19

Prejudice and Discrimination

Yuen J. Huo

> For the people that are now out of work because of the important and necessary containment policies, for instance the shutting down of hotels, bars and restaurants, money will soon be coming to you! The onslaught of the Chinese Virus is not your fault! Will be stronger than ever! (President Donald Trump on Twitter; Coleman, 2020)

> It's not racist at all. No, not at all. It comes from China, that's why. It comes from China. I want to be accurate. (President Donald Trump, White House Coronavirus Task Force News Briefing; Forgey, 2020)

The COVID-19 pandemic has brought about profound changes in the way individuals around the world conduct themselves in their daily lives. One of the more marked changes is the sudden spike in overt hostility towards those perceived as 'outsiders'. In particular, because the spread of COVID-19 started in central China, much of that prejudice has been directed towards the Chinese and, by association, Asians. Indeed, this prejudice has itself spread like a virus around the globe and is particularly evident in the United States. Prior to 2020, President Donald Trump directed his virulent form of nativist politics towards the most vulnerable immigrant group at the time, the Latinx community, calling for a border wall along the US–Mexico border and seeking to deport undocumented migrants from Mexico and other nations in Latin America. However, as the above quotes attest, the COVID-19 pandemic has redirected President Trump's antipathy (and that of his supporters) towards a different racial minority group – Asians.

COVID-19 awakened dormant group-based prejudices

Historically, concerns about contagion have enhanced xenophobia towards foreigners (Rao & Greve Insead, 2018). More generally, fear of the unknown has the capacity not only to inspire new forms of bigotry, but also to foment prejudices that have lain dormant for some time. Especially in times of national distress and uncertainty, outgroups that in better times were viewed in largely positive (albeit rather stereotypical) ways can come to be portrayed in decidedly negative and, indeed, sinister terms. In fourteenth-century Europe, Jews were treated as scapegoats for supposedly carrying the black plague that raced from Asia through the Middle East and Europe. Even after the pandemic was over, they were still persecuted on the basis of false claims that they had helped to spread the illness. Consistent with this reasoning, studies have demonstrated that when dominant groups (e.g., white Canadians, men in STEM) are exposed to demographic projections which suggest that they will become a numerical minority, they feel angrier and more fearful of racial minorities (Outten, Schmitt, Miller, & Garcia, 2012) and less tolerant of these groups (Danbold & Huo, 2017).

The response to COVID-19 in the US provides a clear example of how the sudden onset of acute threat can unleash latent feelings of prejudice. For Asian-Americans, there had been numerous examples of such 'prejudice following crisis' in the country's past. In particular, during World War II, Japanese-Americans were forcibly relocated to internment camps by the US government. In recent decades, such blatant discrimination had abated – with attitudes shifting so that Asian-Americans were seen less as threatening outsiders and instead as a *model minority* (Takaki, 2012). Yet despite these developmental shifts in sentiment, it took just a few weeks for anti-Asian sentiment to be revived during the COVID-19 crisis.

Similar dynamics can be observed in India. Even though Indian minorities played no part in the spread of the virus into the country, here too minorities have found themselves increasingly under attack. In the context of longstanding conflict between Hindus and Muslims, the majority group Hindus have used the COVID-19 crisis to legitimise prejudice and hostility towards the Muslim minority. For example, Ellis-Petersen and Rahman (2020) report that:

> In Mangalore this week, posters started appearing that said Muslims were no longer allowed in certain neighbourhoods. 'No Muslim trader will be allowed access to our hometown until the coronavirus is completely gone,' read a sign in Alape. In the Hindu-dominated village of

> Ankanahalli, a video ... shows Mahesh, the village panchayat president, issuing a warning that if any Hindu in the village is caught fraternising with a Muslim 'you will be fined 500 to 1,000 rupees'.

The speed with which blatant expressions of prejudice against minorities have resurged in the context of the COVID-19 pandemic has taken many by surprise. However, closer analysis suggests that the ingredients for hostility were always present. In the case of Asians, the rise in overt prejudice piggy-backed on the myth of the model minority, which was rooted in the view that Asians are high-achieving, hard-working and accommodating (Fiske, Cuddy, Glick, & Xu 2002). While these attributes are positive, they nevertheless represent stereotypes that overlook individual and subgroup differences within the group (Chao, Chiu, Chan, Mendoza-Denton, & Kwok, 2013). Moreover, the meaning of these stereotypes can be reshaped in ways that construe them as threats to 'ordinary' Americans or Europeans (Oakes et al., 1994). For example, in the context of the massive job losses that have resulted from COVID-19, 'high-achieving' and 'hard-working' may be framed as a manifestation of Asian-Americans' desire to outcompete white Americans or Europeans for the limited jobs that remain.

As a result of these resurgent attitudes, the COVID-19 pandemic has separated those with Asian backgrounds from their fellow nationals along a dormant fault line – this mental division implies that the Asian minority is foreign, or at least less American or European, than whites (Zou & Cheryan, 2017). Indeed, in the US, assessments of both explicit and implicit attitudes show that Asian-Americans are viewed not only as less American than other racial groups, but also as less American than whites from other nations (Devos & Banaji, 2005).

This activation of longstanding foreigner stereotypes is consequential. Shortly after President Trump repeatedly referred to COVID-19 as the 'Chinese' virus, there was a sudden rise in anti-Asian prejudice and hostility. In the first two weeks of launching a website to track anti-Asian discrimination on March 19 2020, Asian and Pacific Islander advocacy coalition A3PCON documented over 1,000 incidents (Jeung, 2020). These incidents ranged from verbal and physical attacks to subtler bias, such as an emergency physician's account of noticing people covering their nose and mouth when they passed him in the hospital hallways (Tavernise & Oppel, 2020). Significantly, reports indicate that this hostility was largely directed towards non-Chinese people, highlighting the tendency for people to view Asian-Americans of different ethnicities as interchangeable (Flores & Huo, 2013), which leaves a much larger group vulnerable to race-based attack. In a context that was framed as 'them' threatening 'us', the outgroup was large and undifferentiated.

Deviation from a group prototype explains prejudice

In order to understand these patterns of growing intolerance towards minorities, it is useful to consider how COVID-19 has triggered social identity concerns specific to the dominant groups in society. It is important to consider that, in nations that are diverse in dimensions of race, ethnicity, religion or language, the dominant group not only holds disproportionate power and status, but also defines the norms of the shared identity against which all members are evaluated. According to the Ingroup Projection Model, all subgroups (including minorities) are evaluated against this norm, and the extent to which they fit the normative expectations of the group (and are thus prototypical of the group) determines their acceptance by the dominant group (Wenzel, Mummendey, & Waldzus, 2007). The more a subgroup deviates from the norms of the shared social category, the more negatively they are evaluated. Members of these groups are also denied access to resources, rights and respectful treatment (Huo, 2002). In contrast, when a group is, in essence, the prototype of the shared social category, its members are evaluated positively. For example, as the most powerful racial group in the US, whites are widely regarded as fitting the prototype of Americans (Devos & Banaji, 2005), and they are therefore judged more positively than other racial groups.

Second, in response to perceived threat, the desire among dominant groups to draw the line between who is normative and who is divergent is intensified. The pretext of 'being different' from the larger group's prototype (and thus the norms that the group holds dear) is used as justification for enhanced group-based discrimination and exclusion. Accordingly, in the US, when primed with information about their group's numerical decline, whites report higher levels of *prototypicality threat*. That is, they become anxious that the association between being white and being American is unravelling (Danbold & Huo, 2015). There is evidence that this threat is experienced by dominant group members as a challenge to their social identity. Specifically, a number of studies demonstrate that a cultural change towards a more complex and inclusive national identity (which potentially challenges the prototype of the group and associated group norms) drives a rise in prejudice and hostility towards immigrants and racial minorities (Danbold & Huo, 2015).

There are reasons to believe that these dynamics have intensified in the face of COVID-19. Here, the resurgence of the 'Asians as foreign' stereotype has amplified delineations of who is a 'true' American or European (whites) and who is not (Asians). In short, because this minority is seen as falling short of the prototype that characterises ingroup identity, it becomes easier for members of the dominant group to justify not just feeling negative about its members, but also acting aggressively towards them. 'They' are no longer part of 'us'. Perhaps 'they' never were.

It is a mistake, however, to assume that there is anything natural or inevitable about this process. In particular, as we saw in Section B, leaders play an active and critical role in defining the contours and norms of ingroup identity (Reicher, Haslam, & Van Bavel, 2019). This means that leaders can either legitimise prejudice against groups they define as threats to the ingroup, or else take steps to discredit any such prejudice. During the COVID-19 crisis the former process has been prominent in the US, where President Trump provided a lightning rod for the negative feelings that some of his supporters already held towards Asian-Americans.

Nevertheless, other countries' leaders went out of their way to model inclusion. For example, in Australia, Prime Minister Scott Morrison reacted angrily to reports of anti-Chinese hostility by pointing to ways in which Chinese-Australians had been exemplary members of the larger Australian community:

> The Chinese-Australian community did an amazing job in those early days of the spread of the coronavirus. They have been an early example to the rest of the country . . . . They showed all Australians back then how to do this. I want to thank them very, very much for the example they set in those early phases. (Fang, Renaldi, & Yang, 2020)

Rather than portraying minority ingroup members as a prototypicality threat, Morrison portrayed them instead as *prototypicality models*.

Prejudice harms its targets

The immediate outcomes of enhanced prejudice and discrimination are clear. The experiences of Asians, long stereotyped as 'foreign' (at least in Western nations), have shifted from simply being reduced to a model minority to becoming the target of escalating micro-aggressions and even outright hostility. Such stigma and discrimination inevitably take their toll on individuals. Experiences with group-based discrimination are reliably associated with a heightened stress response, both physical and psychological (Haslam, Jetten et al., 2018; Matheson & Anisman, 2012). This can lead to a cascade of adverse health outcomes, from depression to obesity and cardiovascular disease (Pascoe & Smart Richman, 2009; see also Chapter 17).

The COVID-19 pandemic has enhanced not only xenophobia towards foreigners, but also prejudice and hostility towards fellow citizens. It is clear that if this goes unchecked, prejudice and intergroup hostility will ultimately have a corrosive effect on the fabric of society. While there is widespread consensus that we must do everything we can to counter attempts to associate COVID-19 with particular groups of people or places, the key questions that remain are not just how to reduce prejudice, but how to work together to build a better society. This is the topic on which our next, and final, chapter focuses.

20

Common Identity and Humanity

John F. Dovidio, Elif G. Ikizer, Jonas R. Kunst and Aharon Levy

> Wearing a mask is a sign of respect. (New York Governor Andrew Cuomo, May 12 2020)

In the first chapter of this book, we discussed the importance of groups with a quote from Andrew Cuomo: "'It's not about me, it's about *we*.' Get your head around the we concept.' Now, in this final chapter, we start with another quotation from the New York Governor illustrating why the 'we concept' (what we would call social identity) is so important.

Responding to COVID-19 is about harnessing the positive side of group psychology

If you make wearing masks a sign of concern for others in the group (a 'we' thing), it becomes a symbol of mutual care and brings people together. However, if you make it about individual beliefs and preferences (an 'I' thing), the mask becomes a symbol of division and a site of conflict. That has been happening across the US, as those who insist on their right to wear masks clash with those who insist on their right not to wear masks (Noor, 2020). It is what led Cuomo to make his remarks. It is also what led another Governor – the Republican Governor of North Dakota, Doug Burgum – to implore citizens not to make masks 'a senseless dividing line' between people. He continued: 'We're all in this together and there's only one battle we're fighting, and that's the battle of the virus' (cited by Pengelly, 2020).

But this issue of mask wearing is not simply a matter of 'we' good, 'I' bad. It is also an issue of how we define the 'we' – or, to put it more formally, it is an issue of how we define the groups to which we belong. Instead of the 'we' referencing all citizens, it can become a matter of 'freedom-loving Conservatives' versus 'public health-concerned Liberals', in which case there is no unity and consensus. Rather, all that one has achieved is collectivised division, rooted in a set of entrenched differences, and hence made more bitter and intractable.

This encapsulates a tension that has run throughout this book. How can we harness the positives of group psychology – solidarity, social support, psychological resilience – without invoking the negatives – division, hatred, conflict? We will start by summarising what has been learnt thus far about these issues before offering a way forward based on what we know about the creation of common identity.

Three lessons emerge from research on intergroup relations

Lesson 1: Threat makes social identity salient and so increases solidarity, cooperation and norm compliance within the group

On whatever else people might differ, few would disagree that we face a life and death struggle against COVID-19. In the first paragraph of Chapter 1, the figures quoted were some 4 million infections and a quarter of a million deaths. That was when the writing started. In the few weeks during which this book has been written, the number of infections has risen by 1.5 million, the number of deaths by 100,000. Whoever we are and wherever we are, COVID-19 represents an existential threat to us all.

If there is one thing that psychologists agree on, even if they sometimes differ on why, it is that threats from outside the group strengthen the salience of social identity (Chapter 7). Within the group, increased social identity salience leads to increased social support, solidarity and adherence to group norms. As we saw in Chapter 11, threatened groups that were already highly cohesive become even more cohesive and, even where there was no previous sense of community, it can often emerge as 'together, we face up to a common threat'. Such loyalty, altruism, community organisation and conformity are crucial in helping us to surmount the psychological and practical problems of a dangerous and uncertain world (Hogg, Abrams, & Brewer, 2017; Kunst, Thomsen, & Dovidio, 2019). This is group psychology at its best.

Lesson 2: Threat consolidates group boundaries and so increases exclusion between groups

A fundamental premise of the social identity approach is that you cannot have an 'us' without a 'them' – for (as we outlined in Chapter 2) how can we have a sense of who we are without contrasting it to those we are not? So, if one strengthens group boundaries, one increases the exclusion of outgroup members as surely as one increases the inclusion of ingroup members.

Nevertheless, this does not necessarily mean that one is always negative towards the outgroup (Jetten, Spears, & Postmes, 2004). For example, scientists may not be poets, but that does not mean that they hate or are in conflict with poets. However, it does mean that scientists are less likely to offer poets the positives (e.g., solidarity and cooperation) which they extend to fellow ingroup members (Reicher et al., 2008).

However, if we see others as a part of the threat to us – especially when it is an existential threat – then the withdrawal of kindness to outgroups can quickly escalate to active cruelty (Reicher et al., 2008; Stephan & Stephan, 2000). When Jewish people were defined as the source of the plague, where Muslims are seen as the source of COVID-19 in India, or Asian-Americans were blamed in the US, then 'their' destruction can be justified in the name of 'our' preservation (see Chapter 19). This is group psychology at its worst.

Lesson 3: Whether we see the best or the worst of group psychology depends upon how inclusively or exclusively we define our ingroups and outgroups

If group threat leads both to solidarity within the group and to exclusion – or even conflict – between groups, then whether we see the best or the worst of group psychology turns on the question of how broadly or narrowly the ingroup is defined. That, in turn, is dependent on how the threat is defined.

If threat is seen to stem from groups *within* the nation, then national unity will be impossible to achieve and domestic conflict will prevail instead. This could be because a particular national minority is accused of being responsible for the disease (as with the notion of 'Corona-Jihadism' in India, which puts blame on

Muslims). However, it could also be because the threat is understood to be not the virus itself but rather the *response* to the virus, and that is blamed on political opponents (as in President Trump's call to 'liberate' states from lockdown imposed by Democratic governors).

If threat is seen to stem from other nations, then international unity will be impossible to achieve and it will be much harder to overcome the pandemic. As Salisbury and Patel (2020) argue, 'responding to Coronavirus needs clarity of global leadership that arches over national interests and is capable of mobilizing resources at a time when economies are facing painful recessions'.

If, however, the threat is defined as the virus itself, and as pitting a non-human source against all of humanity, then there is the possibility of developing what Tajfel and Turner (1979) called the 'superordinate level of categorization'. That is, instead of dividing people into different social categories, humanity as a whole can be constituted as a single category (see also Chapter 7). If that happens, then anyone's suffering becomes our own and we have the prospect of harnessing the best without risking the worst of group psychology.

Overcoming COVID-19 depends on developing a sense of common identity

The crux of our argument is that the best way of harnessing intragroup solidarity without incurring intergroup conflict is to create the broadest and most inclusive ingroups. This idea aligns very much with Gaertner and Dovidio's *common ingroup identity model*. A central premise of this model is that intergroup hostility can be reduced if group members *recategorise* those who would otherwise be seen as outgroup members as ingroup members within an inclusive superordinate category (Gaertner, Dovidio, Guerra, Hehman, & Saguy, 2016). This can happen, for example, when people who are seen as outgroups on the basis of race or ethnicity are recategorised in terms of a shared national identity.

Moreover, research within the common ingroup identity perspective confirms and extends many of the other core points made in this book. When members of previously divided groups come to see themselves as members of a common superordinate category, then erstwhile foes can become fellows. We feel closer to those we once excluded, experience greater empathy for them, engage in greater self-disclosure, and are more accepting and charitable (Dovidio & Banfield, 2015; Dovidio & Gaertner, 2010; Levine & Thompson, 2004). For example, increasing the salience of Jewish students' 'human identity', in contrast to their 'Jewish identity', has been found to enhance their perceptions of similarity between Jews and Germans, as well as their willingness to work constructively with German students (Wohl & Branscombe, 2005).

The critical question, of course, is how this sense of common ingroup identity can be achieved. Again, this is a question we have discussed throughout the book, and again, the common ingroup identity model provides answers that both confirm and extend previous arguments. On the one hand, it is possible to draw on historically established superordinate memberships (e.g., as members of the same local community, organisation, nation or, indeed, as global citizens confronting shared global challenges such as climate change and the fires, floods and droughts it brings across the globe). On the other hand, it is possible to create new inclusive identities forged by common fate or by interdependence in the face of a shared loss or a mutual enemy.

What is more, as argued in Chapter 3, the role of leadership is critical. Whether it be a matter of invoking the relevance of pre-existing categories or of highlighting our interdependence in a dangerous world, leaders mediate between the nature of the world we live in and our understanding of who we are within it. Consider, for instance, the words of European Council President Charles Michel (cited in Barry, 2020): 'This pandemic is putting our societies under serious strain. The well-being of each EU member state depends on the well-being of the whole of the EU. We are all in this together.' His argument centres on the economic interdependence of the individual member states in the EU: one fails, all are in danger. This was a logic picked up by the President of the European Monetary Fund, Ursula von der Leyen, when she presented common European identity as the key mechanism through which Europe could overcome early setbacks in responding to the pandemic – setbacks associated with the fact that 'When Europe really needed an "all for one" spirit, too many initially gave an "only for me" response' (Wheaton & de la Baume, 2020).

Effective responses to COVID-19 require forging an 'all for one' spirit

Our only qualification to von der Leyen's words is that they do not just apply to Europe. The toll from COVID-19 is too high already, aided and abetted by an 'only for me' (or, rather, 'only for my narrow ingroup') spirit. How much further it will rise is highly dependent on our ability to forge an 'all for one' spirit, rooted in the creation of a fully inclusive common group identity.

Epilogue

The themes in this book have been all about the power of the social group. We have shown how we can harness this power to bring us together, to help us work together, to support each other and to remain practically, psychologically and physically strong in the face of COVID-19. At the same time, we have also focused on the need to avoid the dangers of division, hostility and violence. How we move forward is not inscribed in our nature; it is down to the way that we and our leaders construct the boundaries of 'us' and 'them'. Our fate lies in our own hands.

In the previous pages we have outlined the science of social identity. Our hope is that the understandings that this science provides – concerning both the antecedents and consequences of group formation – can guide us towards a better future. But the take-home message can perhaps be expressed more powerfully in poetry. Accordingly, we draw the book to a close with the reflections of 18-year-old Stephen Kiama Ambrose from South Sudan on the nature of the tests that lie ahead of us.

'The human race shall always overcome,' said Jommo Kenyatta

See, I am the ultimate test

How well do you work together?

How well coordinated are you?

*

COVID-19 is my name

I know no boundaries or lanes

No celebrity can match my fame

Like a roaring flame I engulf all on my path

The poor and the rich both feel my wrath

*

You have a common enemy in me

So, lower your guns and focus on me

Lower your rank, tribe, ethnicity and focus on me

For can't you see, can't you see?

I know of no hierarchy

My presence brings fear and anarchy

*

I am stronger than Samson

For I break the unbreakable

I'll break your economy

I'll break your faith

But that's only if you let me

For the racism you show only strengthens me

*

You like hiding your identity, then wear a mask

You claim that your hands are clean, then sanitize

For the death I cause is no man's fault but rather my nature

You shall overcome me; it's in your blood, it's your nature

I am no professor, neither is this a lecture

But only working together can tame my destructive nature

*

As Nations cower in fear

For I grab many victims in a day

For once they see something worse than war

For once they see humanity is worth fighting for

*

What goes up must come down

No authority is higher than me

For I break the laws of traditions

I break the laws of a normal condition

But I'll never break the so-called men

Bend them to their breaking points

Once they kill me, they forget my wrath and once again I'll strike

*

As you suffer because of me

Also try and learn from me and your mistakes

As I go down the books of history

Still there's more to come

Maintain the togetherness

And there will be no harm

Share the little you have

Before I strike and leave you with none

*

The only way to survive me, is by joining heads

Lock your doors for I roam the streets

Stay alert for like an assassin; you never know my target

References

Abbott, A., Nandeibam, S., & O'Shea, L. (2013). Recycling: Social norms and warm-glow revisited. *Ecological Economics*, *90*, 10–18.

ABC News (2020). Coronavirus is killing African-Americans at an alarming rate, but one expert says he is not surprised. *ABC News* (April 16). www.abc.net.au/news/2020-04-16/drum-covid-african-american-affected/12153268

Abrams, D., Randsley de Moura, G., & Travaglino, G. A. (2013). A double standard when group members behave badly: Transgression credit to ingroup leaders. *Journal of Personality and Social Psychology*, *105*, 799–815.

Akerlof, G. A., & Kranton, R. (2010). *Identity economics*. Princeton University Press.

Aldrich, D. P. (2012). Social, not physical, infrastructure: The critical role of civil society after the 1923 Tokyo earthquake. *Disasters*, *36*, 398–419.

Aldrich, D. P. (2013). Rethinking civil society–state relations in Japan after the Fukushima accident. *Polity*, *45*, 249–264.

Aldrich, D. P. (2017). The importance of social capital in building community resilience. In W. Yan & W. Galloway (Eds.), *Rethinking resilience adaptation and transformation in a time of change* (pp. 357–364). Springer.

Allcott, H., Boxell, L., Conway, J. C., Gentzkow, M., Thaler, M., & Yang, D. Y. (2020). Polarization and public health: Partisan differences in social distancing during the coronavirus pandemic. https://doi.org/10.2139/ssrn.3570274

Ardern, J. (2020). Coronavirus: Prime Minister Jacinda Ardern's full COVID-19 speech. *Newshub* (March 23). www.newshub.co.nz/home/politics/2020/03/coronavirus-prime-minister-jacinda-ardern-s-full-COVID-19-speech.html

Arvan, M. (2019). The dark side of morality: Group polarization and moral epistemology. *The Philosophical Forum*, *50*, 87–115.

Asprou, H. (2020). Self-isolating choirs and orchestras are performing powerful at-home concerts during coronavirus outbreak. *Classic FM* (May 7). www.classicfm.com/music-news/coronavirus/self-isolating-choirs-orchestras-perform-concerts/

Assembly of European Regions (2020). COVID-19: A global crisis that requires a collective response. *AER* (April 1). https://aer.eu/COVID-19-a-global-crisis-that-requires-a-collective-response/

Bai, Y., Lin, C-C., Lin, C-Y., Chen, J-Y., Chue, C-M., & Chou, P. (2004). Survey of stress reactions among health care workers involved with the SARS outbreak. *Psychiatric Services*, *55*, 1055–1057.

Baker, N. (2020). The most common conspiracy theories about coronavirus debunked. *SBS News* (May 5). www.sbs.com.au/news/the-most-common-conspiracy-theories-about-coronavirus-debunked

Barron, L. (2020). What we can learn from Singapore, Taiwan and Hong Kong about handling coronavirus. *Time* (March 13). https://time.com/5802293/coronavirus-covid19-singapore-hong-kong-taiwan/

Barrows, S. (1981). *Distorting mirrors*. Yale University Press.

Barry, C. (2020). 'All in this together': EU agrees to budget, recovery plan to beat virus impact. *The Sydney Morning Herald* (April 24). www.smh.com.au/world/europe/all-in-this-together-eu-agrees-budget-recovery-plan-to-beat-virus-impact-20200424-p54msl.html

Beaini, F., & Ulubasoglu, M. (2019). *Demographic profiling: Queensland floods 2010–11 case study Brisbane river catchment area: Optimising post-disaster interventions in Australia*. Bushfire and Natural Hazards CRC.

Bennett, B. (2020). President Trump says Americans should cover their mouths in public – but he won't. *Time* (3 April). https://time.com/5815615/trump-coronavirus-mixed-messaging/

Bennis, W. (1999). The end of leadership: Exemplary leadership is impossible without full inclusion, initiatives, and cooperation of followers. *Organizational Dynamics*, *28*, 71–79.

Bentley, S. V., Cruwys, T., Jetten, J., Crimston, C. R., & Selvanathan, H. P. (2020). Isolated in isolation: The negative impact of social distancing for those already disconnected. Unpublished manuscript: The University of Queensland.

Berkman, L. F., & Syme, S. L. (1979). Social networks, host resistance, and mortality: A nine-year follow-up study of Alameda County residents. *American Journal of Epidemiology*, *109*, 186–204.

Bibby, J., Everest, G., & Abbs, I. (2020). Will COVID-19 be a watershed moment for health inequalities? *The Health Foundation* (May 7). www.health.org.uk/publications/long-reads/will-COVID-19-be-a-watershed-moment-for-health-inequalities

Bilewicz, M., Winiewski, M., Kofta, M., & Wójcik, A. (2013). Harmful ideas: The structure and consequences of anti-semitic beliefs in Poland. *Political Psychology*, *34*, 821–839.

Blader, S. L., & Tyler, T. R. (2009). Testing and extending the group engagement model: Linkages between social identity, procedural justice, economic outcomes, and extra-role behavior. *Journal of Applied Psychology*, *94*, 445–464.

Bonell, C., Michie, S., Reicher, S., West, R., Bear, L., Yardley, L., Curtis, V., Amlôt, R., & Rubin, G. J. (2020). Harnessing behavioural science in public health campaigns to maintain 'social distancing' in response to the COVID-19 pandemic: Key principles. *Journal of Epidemiology and Community Health*. doi: 10.1136/jech-2020-214290

Boseley, S. (2020). 'Absolutely wrong': How UK's coronavirus test strategy unravelled. *The Guardian* (April 1). www.theguardian.com/world/2020/apr/01/absolutely-wrong-how-uk-coronavirus-test-strategy-unravelled

Botner, E. (2018). Impact of a virtual learning program on social isolation for older adults. *Therapeutic Recreation Journal*, *52*, 126–139.

Braddock, I. (2020). Boris Johnson says coronavirus crisis has proved 'there really is such a thing as society' in second update from self-isolation. *Evening Standard* (March 30). www.standard.co.uk/news/politics/boris-johnson-positive-coronavirus-video-update-isolation-a4401166.html

Bradford, B., Hohl, K., Jackson, J., & MacQueen, S. (2015). Obeying the rules of the road: Procedural justice, social identity, and normative compliance. *Journal of Contemporary Criminal Justice*, *31*, 171–191.

Braunack-Mayer, A., Tooher, R., Collins, J. E., Street, J. M., & Marshall, H. (2013). Understanding the school community's response to school closures during the H1N1 2009 influenza pandemic. *BMC Public Health*, *13*, 344.

Bridges, S. (2020). Simon Bridges' full speech on state of emergency. *Newsroom Contributor* (March 25). www.newsroom.co.nz/2020/03/25/1100027/simon-bridges-full-speech-on-state-of-emergency

Bruder, M., Haffke, P., Neave, N., Nouripanah, N., & Imhoff, R. (2013). Measuring individual differences in generic beliefs in conspiracy theories across cultures: The Conspiracy Mentality Questionnaire (CMQ). *Frontiers in Psychology*, *4*, Article *225*, 1–15.

Bump, P. (2020). The circumstances are wildly different. Trump's response is the same. *The Washington Post* (April 6). www.washingtonpost.com/politics/2020/04/05/circumstances-are-wildly-different-trumps-response-is-same/

Burcusa, S. L., & Iacono, W. G. (2007). Risk for recurrence of depression. *Clinical Psychology Review*, *27*, 959–985.

Butchireddygari, L. (2020). How concerned are Americans about coronavirus so far? *Five Thirty Eight* (March 13). https://fivethirtyeight.com/features/how-concerned-are-americans-about-coronavirus-so-far/

Butler, P. (2020). NHS coronavirus crisis volunteers frustrated at lack of tasks. *The Guardian* (May 3). www.theguardian.com/world/2020/may/03/nhs-coronavirus-crisis-volunteers-frustrated-at-lack-of-tasks?CMP=Share_iOSApp_Other

Camus, A. (1947). *The plague* (S. Gilbert, Trans.). The Modern Library.

Carrell, C. (2020). Scotland's chief medical officer quits over second home row. *The Guardian* (April 6). www.theguardian.com/uk-news/2020/apr/05/scotland-chief-medical-officer-seen-flouting-lockdown-advice-catherine-calderwood

Carter, H., & Amlôt, R. (2016). Mass casualty decontamination guidance and psychosocial aspects of CBRN incident management: A review and synthesis. *PLOS Currents*, *8*.

Carter, H., Drury, J., & Amlôt, R. (2018). Social identity and intergroup relationships in the management of crowds during mass emergencies and disasters: Recommendations for emergency planners and responders. *Policing: A Journal of Policy and Practice*. doi:10.1093/police/pay013

Carter, H., Drury, J., Amlôt, R., Rubin, G. J., & Williams, R. (2015). Effective responder communication, perceived responder legitimacy and group identification predict public cooperation and compliance in a mass decontamination visualisation experiment. *Journal of Applied Social Psychology*, *45*, 173–189.

Carter, H., Drury, J., Rubin, G. J., Williams, R., & Amlôt, R. (2014). Effective responder communication improves efficiency and psychological outcomes in a mass decontamination field experiment: Implications for public behaviour in the event of a chemical incident. *PLOS One*, *9*, e89846.

Carter, H., Drury, J., Rubin, G. J., Williams, R., & Amlôt, R. (2015). Applying crowd psychology to develop recommendations for the management of mass decontamination. *Health Security*, *13*, 45–53.

Castano, E., Yzerbyt, V., Paladino, M.-P., & Sacchi, S. (2002). I belong, therefore, I exist: Ingroup identification, ingroup entitativity, and ingroup bias. *Personality and Social Psychology Bulletin*, *28*, 135–143.

Cha, A. E. (2020). A funeral and a birthday party: CDC traces Chicago coronavirus outbreak to two family gatherings. *Washington Post* (April 9). www.washingtonpost.com/health/2020/04/08/funeral-birthday-party-hugs-COVID-19/

Chao, M. M., Chiu, C. Y., Chan, W., Mendoza-Denton, R., & Kwok, C. (2013). The model minority as a shared reality and its implication for interracial perceptions. *Asian American Journal of Psychology*, *4*, 84–92.

Charles, M. (2019). ComeUnity and community in the face of impunity. In D. Bulley, J. Edkins, & N. El-Enany (Eds.), *After Grenfell: Violence, resistance and response* (pp. 167–192). Pluto Press.

Chik, H., & Lew, L. (2020). Fact vs fiction: Timeline of a coronavirus war of words between Beijing and Washington. *South China Morning Post* (March 25). www.scmp.com/news/china/politics/article/3076800/fact-vs-fiction-timeline-coronavirus-war-words-between-beijing

Chung, R. Y. N., Dong, D., & Li, M. M. (2020). Socioeconomic gradient in health and the COVID-19 outbreak. *BMJ, 369*.

CIA (2000). The CIA's assessment of threat infectious disease. *Executive Intelligence Review, 27*, 69–72.

Cialdini, R. B. (1984). *Influence: The new psychology of modern persuasion.* Quill.

Cialdini, R. B., Demaine, L. J., Sagarin, B. J., Barrett, D. W., Rhoads, K., & Winter, P. L. (2006). Managing social norms for persuasive impact. *Social Influence, 1*, 3–15.

Cialdini, R. B., & Goldstein, N. J. (2004). Social influence: Compliance and conformity. *Annual Review of Psychology, 55*, 591–621.

Cialdini, R. B., Reno, R. R., & Kallgren, C. A. (1990). A focus theory of normative conduct: Recycling the concept of norms to reduce littering in public places. *Journal of Personality and Social Psychology, 58*, 1015–1026.

Cohen, S., Doyle, W. J., Turner, R., Alper, C. M., & Skoner, D. P. (2003). Sociability and susceptibility to the common cold. *Psychological Science, 1*, 389–395.

Cohn Jr, S. K. (2007). The Black Death and the burning of Jews. *Past and Present, 196*, 3–36.

Cohn Jr, S. K. (2018). *Epidemics: Hate and compassion from the plague of Athens to AIDS.* Oxford University Press.

Coleman, J. (2020). Trump promises help for Americans out of work because of virus. *The Hill* (March 18). https://thehill.com/policy/finance/488170-trump-promises-help-for-people-out-of-work-because-of-virus

College of Policing (2020). Explain, Engage, Encourage, Enforce – applying the four 'E's. www.college.police.uk/What-we-do/COVID-19/Documents/Engage-Explain-Encourage-Enforce-guidance.pdf

Conn, D., Lawrence, F., Lewis, P., Carrell, S., Pegg, D., Davies, H., & Evans, R. (2020). Revealed: The inside story of the UK's COVID-19 crisis. *The Guardian* (April 30). www.theguardian.com/world/2020/apr/29/revealed-the-inside-story-of-uk-COVID-19-coronavirus-crisis

Cook, K. S., Yamagishi, T., Cheshire, C., Cooper, R., Matsuda, M., & Mashima, R. (2014). Trust building via risk taking: A cross-societal experiment. *Social Psychology Quarterly, 68*, 121–142.

Crimston, C. R., Selvanathan, H. P., & Jetten, J. (2020). Moral polarization predicts support for a strong leader via the perceived breakdown of society. Unpublished manuscript: The University of Queensland.

Cruwys, T., Dingle, G. A., Haslam, C., Haslam, S. A., Jetten, J., & Morton, T. (2013). Social group memberships protect against future depression, alleviate depression symptoms and prevent depression relapse. *Social Science & Medicine*, *98*, 179–186.

Cruwys, T., Greenaway, K., Ferris, L. J., Rathbone, J. A., Saeri, A. K., Williams, E., Parker, S. L., Chang, M. X-L., Croft, N., Bingley, W., & Grace, L. (2020). When trust goes wrong: A social identity model of risk taking. *Journal of Personality and Social Psychology*. doi: 10.1037/pspi0000243

Cruwys, T., Norwood, R., Chachay, V. S., Ntontis, E., & Sheffield, J. (2020). 'An important part of who I am': The predictors of dietary adherence among weight-loss, vegetarian, vegan, paleo, and gluten-free dietary groups. *Nutrients*, *12*, 970–986.

Cruwys, T., Saeri, A. K., Radke, H. R. M., Walter, Z. C., Crimston, D., & Ferris, L. J. (2019). Risk and protective factors for mental health at a youth mass gathering. *European Child and Adolescent Psychiatry*, *28*, 211–222.

Cruwys, T., South, E. I., Greenaway, K. H. & Haslam, S. A. (2015). Social identity reduces depression by fostering positive attributions. *Social Psychological and Personality Science*, *6*, 65–74.

Curtis, V., de Barra, M., & Aunger, R. (2011). Disgust as an adaptive system for disease avoidance behaviour. *Philosophical Transactions of the Royal Society of London. Series B: Biological Sciences*, *366*, 389–401.

D'Urso, J. (2020). Here's why some pictures of people supposedly breaking coronavirus social distancing rules can be misleading. *BuzzFeed News* (April 28). www.buzzfeed.com/joeydurso/coronavirus-social-distancing-lockdown-photos

Danbold, F., & Huo, Y. J. (2015). No longer 'all-American'? Whites' defensive reactions to their numerical decline. *Social Psychological and Personality Science*, *6*, 210–218.

Danbold, F., & Huo, Y. J. (2017). Men's defense of their prototypicality undermines the success of women in STEM initiatives. *Journal of Experimental Social Psychology*, *72*, 57–66.

Davidson, J. (2020). The leader of the free world gives a speech, and she nails it. *New York Magazine* (March 18). https://nymag.com/intelligencer/2020/03/angela-merkel-nails-coronavirus-speech-unlike-trump.html

Davis, N. Z. (1973). The rites of violence: Religious riot in sixteenth-century France. *Past & Present*, *59*, 51–91.

Delello, J. A., & McWhorter, R. R. (2015). Reducing the digital divide: Connecting older adults to iPad technology. *Journal of Applied Gerontology*, *36*, 3–28.

Devos, T., & Banaji, M. R. (2005). American = white? *Journal of Personality and Social Psychology*, *88*, 447–466.

Dirks, K. T., & Skarlicki, D. P. (2004). Trust in leaders: Existing research and emerging issues. In R. M. Kramer & K. S. Cook (Eds.), *Trust and distrust in organizations: Dilemmas and approaches* (pp. 21–40). Russell Sage Foundation.

Douglas, K., & Sutton, R. M. (2018). Why conspiracy theories matter: A social psychological analysis. *European Review of Social Psychology, 29*, 256–298.

Douglas, K., Sutton, R. M., Callan, M. J., Dawtry, R. J., & Harvey, R. J. (2016). Someone is pulling the strings: Hypersensitive agency detection and belief in conspiracy theories. *Thinking & Reasoning, 22*, 57–77.

Dovidio, J. F., & Banfield, J. C. (2015). Intergroup cooperation. In D. A. Schroeder & W. Graziano (Eds.), *The Oxford handbook of prosocial behavior* (pp. 562–581). Oxford University Press.

Dovidio, J. F., & Gaertner, S. L. (2010). Intergroup bias. In S. T. Fiske, D. Gilbert, & G. Lindzey (Eds.), *Handbook of social psychology* (5th ed., Vol. 2, pp. 1084–1121). Wiley.

Drury, J. (2012). Collective resilience in mass emergencies and disasters. In J. Jetten, C. Haslam, & S. A. Haslam (Eds.), *The social cure: Identity, health and well-being* (pp. 195–215). Psychology Press.

Drury, J., Carter, H., Cocking, C., Ntontis, E., Guven, S. T., & Amlôt, R. (2019). Facilitating collective resilience in the public in emergencies: Twelve recommendations based on the social identity approach. *Frontiers in Public Health, 7*, 1–21.

Drury, J., Novelli, D., & Stott, C. (2013). Psychological disaster myths in the perception and management of mass emergencies. *Journal of Applied Social Psychology, 43*, 2259–2270.

Drury, J., Novelli, D., & Stott, C. (2015). Managing to avert disaster: Explaining collective resilience at an outdoor music event. *European Journal of Social Psychology, 45*, 533–547.

Dujardin, A. (2020). Vandaag is de intelligente lockdown een maand van kracht: Het kabinet heeft burgers onderschat (The intelligent lockdown has been in effect for a month: The cabinet has underestimated citizens). *Trouw* (April 12). www.trouw.nl/binnenland/vandaag-is-de-intelligente-lockdown-een-maand-van-kracht-het-kabinet-heeft-burgers-onderschat~b1f34508/?referer=https%3A%2F%2Fwww.google.com.au%2F

Duncan, G. (2020). New Zealand's coronavirus elimination strategy has united a nation. Can that unity outlast lockdown? *The Conversation* (April 15). https://theconversation.com/new-zealands-coronavirus-elimination-strategy-has-united-a-nation-can-that-unity-outlast-lockdown-135040

Ellemers, N. (1993). The influence of socio-structural variables on identity enhancement strategies. *European Review of Social Psychology, 4*, 27–57.

Ellemers, N., Spears, R., & Doosje, B. (1997). Sticking together or falling apart: In-group identification as a psychological determinant of group commitment versus individual mobility. *Journal of Personality and Social Psychology*, *72*, 617–626.

Ellis-Petersen, H. & Rahman, S. A. (2020). Coronavirus conspiracy theories targeting Muslims spread in India. *The Guardian* (April 13). www.theguardian.com/world/2020/apr/13/coronavirus-conspiracy-theories-targeting-muslims-spread-in-india

Enders, A. M., & Armaly, M. T. (2019). The differential effects of actual and perceived polarization. *Political Behavior*, *41*, 815–839.

Engelen, B., & Schmidt, A. (2020). The ethics of nudging: An overview. *Philosophy Compass*, Article e12658.

Erikson, K. T. (1976/2006). *Everything in its path: Destruction of community in the Buffalo Creek flood*. Simon & Schuster.

European Federation of Psychologists' Associations (EFPA) Standing Committee for Geropsychology (2020). EFPA position statement on COVID-19 related health advice for older adults. *EFPA* (March 24). http://efpa.eu/COVID-19/health-advice-for-older-adults

Evans, E. J. (2004). *Thatcher and Thatcherism: The making of the contemporary world*. Routledge.

Fang, J., Renaldi, E., & Yang, S. (2020). Australians urged to 'show kindness' amid reports of COVID-19 racial discrimination complaints. *ABC News* (April 3). www.abc.net.au/news/2020-04-03/racism-COVID-19-coronavirus-outbreak-commissioner-discrimination/12117738

Fehr, E., & Fischbacher, U. (2004). Social norms and human cooperation. *Trends in Cognitive Sciences*, *8*, 185–190.

Fink, S. (2020). Worst-case estimates for U.S. coronavirus deaths. *New York Times* (March 13). www.nytimes.com/2020/03/13/us/coronavirus-deaths-estimate.html

Firing, K., & Laberg, J. C. (2012). Personal characteristics and social identity as predictors of risk taking among military officers: An empirical study. *International Journal of Management*, *29*, 86–98.

Fiske, S. T., Cuddy, A. J. C., Glick, P., & Xu, J. (2002). A model of (often mixed) stereotype content: Competence and warmth respectively follow from perceived status and competition. *Journal of Personality and Social Psychology*, *82*, 878–902.

Fiske, S. T., & Taylor, S. E. (1984). *Social cognition*. Random House.

Flores, N. M., & Huo, Y. J. (2013). 'We' are not all alike: Consequences of neglecting national origin identities among Asians and Latinos. *Social Psychological and Personality Science*, *4*, 143–150.

Forgey, Q. (2020). Trump on 'Chinese virus' label: 'It's not racist at all'. *Politico* (March 18). www.politico.com/news/2020/03/18/trump-pandemic-drumbeat-coronavirus-135392

FR24News (2020). Coronavirus chaos: More than 350,000 people fined after breaking lock laws. *FR24News* (April 2). www.fr24news.com/a/2020/04/france-coronavirus-chaos-more-than-350000-people-fined-after-breaking-lock-laws-world-new.html

Fritsche, I., Jonas, E., Ablasser, C., Beyer, M., Kuban, J., Manger, A., & Schultz, M. (2013). The power of we: Evidence for group-based control. *Journal of Experimental Social Psychology*, *49*, 19–32.

Fuentes, V. (2020). Protests over food shortages erupt in Chile amid virus lockdown. *Bloomberg* (May 19). www.bloomberg.com/news/articles/2020-05-19/protests-over-food-shortages-erupt-in-chile-amid-virus-lockdown

Gabbatt, A. (2020). 'We have a responsibility': Fox News declares coronavirus a crisis in abrupt U-turn. *The Guardian* (March 17). www.theguardian.com/media/2020/mar/17/fox-news-coronavirus-outbreak-trump

Gaertner, S. L., Dovidio, J. F., Guerra, R., Hehman, E., & Saguy, T. (2016). A common ingroup identity: A categorization-based approach for reducing intergroup bias. In T. Nelson (Ed.), *Handbook of prejudice, discrimination, and stereotyping* (2nd ed., pp. 433–454). Psychology Press.

Gallagher, S., Meaney, S., & Muldoon, O. T. (2014). Social identity influences stress appraisals and cardiovascular reactions to acute stress exposure. *British Journal of Health Psychology*, *19*, 566–579.

Gardner, P. J., & Moallef, P. (2015). Psychological impact on SARS survivors: Critical review of the English language literature. *Canadian Psychology/Psychologie Canadienne*, *56*, 123–135.

Gerber, J., & Wheeler, L. (2009). On being rejected: A meta-analysis of experimental research on rejection. *Perspectives on Psychological Science*, *4*, 468–488.

Gerst-Emerson, K., & Jayawardhana, J. (2015). Loneliness as a public health issue: The impact of loneliness on health care utilization among older adults. *American Journal of Public Health*, *105*, 1013–1019.

Giessner, S. R., & van Knippenberg, D. (2008). 'License to fail': Goal definition, leader group prototypicality, and perceptions of leadership effectiveness after leader failure. *Organizational Behavior and Human Decision Processes*, *105*, 14–35.

Gigerenzer, G. (2018). The bias bias in behavioral economics. *Review of Behavioral Economics*, *5*, 303–336.

Giner, S. (1976). *Mass society*. Martin Robertson.

Gleibs, I., Haslam, C., Jones, J., Haslam, S. A., McNeil, J., & Connolly, H. (2011). No country for old men? The role of a Gentlemen's Club in promoting social engagement and psychological well-being in residential care. *Aging and Mental Health, 15*, 456–466.

Goertzel, T. (1994). Belief in conspiracy theories. *Political Psychology, 15*, 731–742.

Goertzel, T. (2010). Conspiracy theories in science. *EMBO Reports, 11*, 493–499.

Google Trends (2020). https://trends.google.com/trends/explore?date=today%20 5-y&q=loneliness

Greenaway, K. H., & Cruwys, T. (2015). The threat within: The source of a threat to group determines its effects. Unpublished data: University of Melbourne.

Greenaway, K. H., & Cruwys, T. (2019). The source model of group threat: Responding to internal and external threats. *American Psychologist, 74*, 218–231.

Greenaway, K. H., Haslam, S. A., & Bingley, W. (2019). Are 'they' out to get me? A social identity model of paranoia. *Group Processes & Intergroup Relations, 22*, 984–1001.

Greenaway, K. H., Louis, W. R., Hornsey, M. J., & Jones, J. M. (2014). Perceived control qualifies the effects of threat on prejudice. *British Journal of Social Psychology, 53*, 422–442.

Greenaway, K. H., Saeri, A. K., & Cruwys, T. (2020). Why are we calling it 'social distancing'? Right now, we need social connections more than ever. *The Conversation* (24 March). https://theconversation.com/why-are-we-calling-it-social-distancing-right-now-we-need-social-connections-more-than-ever-134249

Greenaway, K. H., Wright, R. G., Willingham, J., Reynolds, K. J., & Haslam, S. A. (2015). Shared identity is key to effective communication. *Personality and Social Psychology Bulletin, 41*, 171–82.

Greenhalgh, T., Schmid, M. B., Czypionka, T., Bassler, D., & Gruer, L. (2020). Face masks for the public during the COVID-19 crisis. *BMJ, 369*.

Hahn, U., Chater, N., Lagnado, D., & Osman, M. (2020). Open letter to the UK government regarding COVID-19 (March 16). https://sites.google.com/view/covidopenletter/home

Hall, J. A. (2018). When is social media use social interaction? Defining mediated social interaction. *New Media & Society, 20*, 162–179.

Hammer, J. C., Fisher, J. D., Fitzgerald, P., & Fisher, W. A. (1996). When two heads aren't better than one: AIDS risk behavior in college-age couples. *Journal of Applied Social Psychology, 26*, 375–397.

Hancock, M. (2020). United Kingdom COVID-19 Briefing Transcript April 5. *Rev Transcript Library* (April 5). www.rev.com/blog/transcripts/united-kingdom-COVID-19-briefing-transcript-april-5

Harrison, M. (2012). *Contagion: How commerce has spread disease.* Yale University Press.

Hartner, M., Kirchler, E., Poschalko, A., & Rechberger, S. (2010). Taxpayers' compliance by procedural and interactional fairness perceptions and social identity. *Journal of Psychology & Economics, 3*, 12–31.

Haslam, C., Cruwys, T., Chang, M. X-L., Bentley, S. V., Haslam, S. A., Dingle, G. A., & Jetten, J. (2019). Groups 4 Health reduces loneliness and social anxiety in adults with psychological distress: Findings from a randomized controlled trial. *Journal of Consulting and Clinical Psychology, 87*, 787–801.

Haslam, C., Cruwys, T., & Haslam, S. A. (2014). 'The we's have it': Evidence for the distinctive benefits of group engagement in enhancing cognitive health in ageing. *Social Science & Medicine, 120*, 57–66.

Haslam, C., Haslam, S. A., Jetten, J., Cruwys, T., & Steffens, N. K. (2020). Life change, social identity, and health. *Annual Review of Psychology*.

Haslam, C., Haslam, S. A., Ysseldyk, R., McCloskey, L.-G., Pfisterer, K., & Brown, S. G. (2014). Social identification moderates cognitive health and well-being following story- and song-based reminiscence. *Aging and Mental Health, 18*, 425–434.

Haslam, C., Jetten, J., Cruwys, T., Dingle, G. A., & Haslam, S. A. (2018). *The new psychology of health: Unlocking the social cure*. Routledge.

Haslam, S. A. (2001). *Psychology in organizations: The social identity approach* (2nd ed.). Sage.

Haslam, S. A., Haslam, C., & Cruwys, T. (2019). Loneliness is a social cancer, every bit as alarming as cancer itself. *The Conversation* (November 19). https://theconversation.com/lonelines-is-a-social-cancer-every-bit-as-alarming-as-cancer-itself-126741

Haslam, S. A., McMahon, C., Cruwys, T., Haslam, C., Greenaway, K. H., Jetten, J., & Steffens, N. K. (2018). Social cure, what social cure? The propensity to underestimate the importance of social factors for health. *Social Science & Medicine, 198*, 14–21.

Haslam, S. A., & Reicher, S. D. (2006). Stressing the group: Social identity and the unfolding dynamics of responses to stress. *Journal of Applied Psychology, 91*, 1037–1052.

Haslam, S. A., & Reicher, S. D. (2017). 50 years of 'obedience to authority': From blind conformity to engaged followership. *Annual Review of Law and Social Science, 13*, 59–78.

Haslam, S. A., Reicher, S. D., & Birney, M. E. (2014). Nothing by mere authority: Evidence that in an experimental analogue of the Milgram paradigm participants are motivated not by orders but by appeals to science. *Journal of Social Issues, 70*, 473–488.

Haslam, S. A., Reicher, S. D., & Platow, M. J. (2011). *The new psychology of leadership: Identity, influence, and power*. Psychology Press.

Haslam, S. A., & Turner, J. C. (1992). Context-dependent variation in social stereotyping 2: The relationship between frame of reference, self-categorization and accentuation. *European Journal of Social Psychology, 22*, 251–277.

Hawkley L. C., & Cacioppo, J. T. (2003). Loneliness and pathways to disease. *Brain, Behavior and Immunity, 17*, 98–105.

Hawley, S. (2020). Coronavirus in Spain is 'frightening on every level': So how did things get so bad there? *ABC News* (April 1). www.abc.net.au/news/2020-04-01/spains-coronavirus-reality-is-grim-how-did-it-start-there/12103590

Hawryluck, L., Gold, W. L., Robinson, S., Pogorski, S., Galea, S., & Styra, R. (2004). SARS control and psychological effects of quarantine, Toronto, Canada. *Emerging Infectious Diseases, 10*, 1206–1212.

Heath, B. (2020). Americans divided on party lines over risk from coronavirus: Reuters/Ipsos poll. *Reuters* (March 7). www.reuters.com/article/us-health-coronavirus-usa-polarization/americans-divided-on-party-lines-over-risk-from-coronavirus-reuters-ipsos-poll-idUSKBN20T2O3

Helsloot, I., & Ruitenberg, A. (2004). Citizen response to disasters: A survey of literature and some practical implications. *Journal of Contingencies and Crisis Management, 12*, 98–111.

Hilton, D., Levine, A., & Zanetis, J. (2019). Don't lose the connection: Virtual visits for older adults. *Journal of Museum Education, 44*, 253–263.

Hogg, M. A. (2001). A social identity theory of leadership. *Personality and Social Psychology Review, 5*, 184–200.

Hogg, M. A., Abrams, D., & Brewer, M. B. (2017). Social identity: The role of self in group processes and intergroup relations. *Group Processes & Intergroup Relations, 20*, 570–581.

Holroyd, M. (2020). Coronavirus: Dutch PM appoints opposition minister as new Health Secretary. *Euronews* (March 20). www.euronews.com/2020/03/20/coronavirus-dutchpm-appoints-opposition-minister-as-new-health-secretary

Holt-Lunstad, J., Smith, T. B., & Layton, J. B. (2010). Social relationships and mortality risk: A meta-analytic review. *PLoS Med, 7*, e1000316.

Hopkins, N., Reicher, S., Stevenson, C., Pandey, K., Shankar, S., & Tewari, S. (2019). Social relations in crowds: Recognition, validation and solidarity. *European Journal of Social Psychology, 49*, 1283–1297.

Hornsey, M. J., & Fielding, K. S. (2017). Attitude roots and Jiu Jitsu persuasion: Understanding and overcoming the motivated rejection of science. *American Psychologist, 72*, 459–473.

Horowitz, J., Bubola, E., & Povoledo, E. (2020). Italy, pandemic's new epicenter, has lessons for the world. *New York Times* (March 21). www.nytimes.com/2020/03/21/world/europe/italy-coronavirus-center-lessons.html

Hudson, A. (2020). COVID-19 has unleashed 'tsunami of hate and scaremongering,' says U.N. chief. *Newsweek* (May 8). www.newsweek.com/COVID-19-has-unleashed-tsunami-hate-scaremongering-says-un-chief-1502740

Hult Khazaie, D., & Khan, S. S. (2019). Shared social identification in mass gatherings lowers health risk perceptions via lowered disgust. *British Journal of Social Psychology*. doi: 10.1111/bjso.12362

Huo, Y. J. (2002). Justice and the regulation of social relations: When and why do group members deny claims to social goods? *British Journal of Social Psychology, 41*, 535–562.

Ingram, I., Kelly, P. J., Deane, F. P., Baker, A. L., Goh, M. C. W., Raftery, D. K., & Dingle, G. A. (2020). Loneliness among people with substance use problems: A narrative systematic review. *Drug and Alcohol Review*. doi: 10.1111/dar.13064

Jackson, J., Posch, C., Bradford, B., Hobson, Z., Kyprianides, A., & Yesberg, J. (2020). The lockdown and social norms: Why the UK is complying by consent rather than compulsion. *LSE Blogs* (April 27). https://blogs.lse.ac.uk/politicsandpolicy/lockdown-social-norms/

Jetten, J., Bentley, S. V., Crimston, C. R., Selvanathan, H. P., Steffens, N. K., Haslam, C., Haslam, S. A., & Cruwys, T. (2020). How COVID-19 affects our social life. Unpublished data: The University of Queensland.

Jetten, J., Fielding, K. S., Crimston, C., Mols, F., & Haslam, S. A. (2020). Responding to climate change disaster: The case of the 2019/2020 bushfires in Australia. Unpublished manuscript: The University of Queensland.

Jetten, J., Haslam, C., & Haslam, S. A. (Eds.). (2012). *The social cure: Identity, health and well-being*. Psychology Press.

Jetten, J., Haslam, C., Haslam, S. A., Dingle, G., & Jones, J. J. (2014). How groups affect our health and well-being: The path from theory to policy. *Social Issues and Policy Review, 8*, 103–130.

Jetten, J., & Peters, K. (Eds.). (2019). *The social psychology of inequality*. Springer.

Jetten, J., Spears, R., & Postmes, T. (2004). Intergroup distinctiveness and differentiation: A meta-analytic integration. *Journal of Personality and Social Psychology, 86*, 862–879.

Jetten, J., Wang, Z., Steffens, N. K., Mols, F., Peters, K., & Verkuyten, M. (2017). A social identity analysis of responses to economic inequality. *Current Opinion in Psychology, 18*, 1–5.

Jeung, R. (2020). *Incidents of coronavirus discrimination* March 26–April 1, 2020: A report for A3PCON AND CAA. www.asianpacificpolicyandplanning-council.org/wp-content/uploads/Press_Release_4_3_20.pdf

Jimenez, P., & Iyer, G. S. (2016). Tax compliance in a social setting: The influence of social norms, trust in government, and perceived fairness on taxpayer compliance. *Advances in Accounting, 34*, 17–26.

Johns Hopkins University (2020). *Coronavirus resource centre*. https://corona virus.jhu.edu/map.html

Johnson, B. (2020). Coronavirus: Boris Johnson's address to the nation in full. *British Broadcasting Corporation* (March 23). www.bbc.com/news/uk-52011928

Johnson, C. (2020). Has coronavirus killed ideology? No, it's just cycled it around again. *The Conversation* (April 20). https://theconversation.com/has-coronavirus-killed-ideology-no-its-just-cycled-it-around-again-136615

Jolley, D., Douglas, K., & Sutton, R. M. (2018). Blaming a few bad apples to save a threatened barrel: The system-justifying function of conspiracies. *Political Psychology*, *39*, 465–478.

Jolley, D., Meleady, R., & Douglas, K. (2020). Exposure to intergroup conspiracy theories promotes prejudice which spreads across groups. *British Journal of Psychology*, *111*, 17–35.

Jones, A. (2020). We are living in the age of hysteria. *Sky News* (March 4). www.youtube.com/watch?v=wUrnYZiKZkA

Kahneman, D. (2011). *Thinking, fast and slow*. Farrar, Straus and Giroux.

Kaonga, G. (2020). India chaos erupts on streets as thousands of migrants clash with police in horror video. *Daily Express* (April 14). www.express.co.uk/news/world/1268858/India-News-migrant-video-protest-police-clash-coronavirus-lockdown-latest-Bandra-riots

Kearns, M., Muldoon, O. T., Msetfi, R. M., & Surgenor, P. W. (2017). Darkness into light? Identification with the crowd at a suicide prevention fundraiser promotes well-being amongst participants. *European Journal of Social Psychology*, *47*, 878–888.

Kelley, R. E. (1988). In praise of followers. *Harvard Business Review*, *66*, 142–148.

Kinsella, E. L., Muldoon, O. T., Fortune, D. G., & Haslam, C. (2018). Collective influences on individual functioning: Multiple group memberships, self-regulation, and depression after acquired brain injury. *Neuropsychological Rehabilitation*, *22*, 1–15.

Kinsey, M. J., Gwynne, S. M. V., Kuligowski, E. D., & Kinateder, M. (2019). Cognitive biases within decision making during fire evacuations. *Fire Technology*, *55*, 465–485.

Klopp, J. (2020). Message to Liverpool supporters. *Liverpool Football Club Website* (March 13). www.liverpoolfc.com/news/first-team/390397-jurgen-klopp-message-to-supporters

Kluth, A. (2020). COVID-19 will lead to social unrest, revolutions. *New Straits Times* (April 12). www.nst.com.my/opinion/columnists/2020/04/583549/COVID-19-will-lead-social-unrest-revolutions

Knight, C., Haslam, S. A., & Haslam, C. (2010). In home or at home? Evidence that collective decision making enhances older adults' social identification, well-being and use of communal space when moving to a new care facility. *Ageing & Society, 30*, 1393–1418.

Kristof, N. (2020). Crumbs for the hungry but windfalls for the rich. *New York Times* (May 23). www.nytimes.com/2020/05/23/opinion/sunday/coronavirus-economic-response.html?

Kuiper, J. S., Zuidersma, M., Oude Vashaar, R. C., Zuidema, S. U., van den Heuvel, E. R., Stolk, R. P., & Smidt, N. (2015). Social relationships and risk of dementia: A systematic review and meta-analysis of longitudinal cohort studies. *Ageing Research Reviews, 22*, 39–57.

Kunst, J. R., Thomsen, L., & Dovidio, J. F. (2019). Divided loyalties: Perceptions of disloyalty underpin bias toward dually-identified minority-group members. *Journal of Personality and Social Psychology, 117*, 807–838.

Lam, C. (2020). Cooking is helping Australian families stay connected to their cultures during lockdown. *SBS* (April 18). www.sbs.com.au/news/cooking-is-helping-australian-families-stay-connected-to-their-cultures-during-lockdown

Le Bon, G. (1895/1960). *The crowd: A study of the popular mind*. Reprinted by Viking.

Leaders League (2020). Mixed approval rating fortunes for world leaders during COVID-19 (April 10). www.leadersleague.com/en/news/mixed-approval-rating-fortunes-for-world-leaders-during-COVID-19

Levine, M., & Manning, R. (2013). Social identity, group processes, and helping in emergencies. *European Review of Social Psychology, 24*, 225–251.

Levine, M., Prosser, A., Evans, D., & Reicher, S. (2005). Identity and emergency intervention: How social group membership and inclusiveness of group boundaries shape helping behavior. *Personality and Social Psychology Bulletin, 31*, 443–453.

Levine, R. M., & Thompson, K. (2004). Identity, place and bystander intervention: Social categories and helping after natural disasters. *Journal of Social Psychology, 144*, 229–245.

Levy, A. (2020). Coronavirus: How times of crisis reveal our emotional connection with strangers. *The Conversation* (May 15). https://theconversation.com/coronavirus-how-times-of-crisis-reveal-our-emotional-connection-with-strangers-136652

Lewandowsky, S., Ecker, U. K. H., Seifert, C. M., Schwarz, N., & Cook, J. (2012). Misinformation and its correction: Continued influence and successful debiasing. *Psychological Science in the Public Interest, 13*, 106–131.

Liddy, M., Hanrahan, C., & Byrd, J. (2020). How Australians feel about the coronavirus crisus and Scott Morrison's response. *ABC News* (April 28).

www.abc.net.au/news/2020-04-28/coronavirus-data-feelings-opinions-covid-survey-numbers/12188608

Liu, J. H., & Hilton, D. J. (2005). How the past weighs on the present: Social representations of history and their role in identity politics. *British Journal of Social Psychology*, *44*, 537–556.

Lowery, M. (2016). *They can't kill us all*. Hachette USA.

Luscombe, B. (2020). Why overreacting to the threat of the coronavirus may be rational. *Time* (March 11). https://time.com/5801010/coronavirus-overreaction/

Mackey, R. (2020). Through creative accounting, Trump tries to cast America's death toll as an achievement. *The Intercept* (May 3). https://theintercept.com/2020/05/02/creative-accounting-trump-tries-cast-americas-death-toll-achievement/

Maguire, E. R., Khade, N., & Mora, V. (2020). Improve the policing of crowds. In C. M. Katz & E. R. Maguire (Eds.), *Transforming the police: Thirteen key reforms* (pp. 235–248). Waveland Press.

March, E., & Springer, J. (2019). Belief in conspiracy theories: The predictive role of schizotypy, Machiavellianism, and primary psychopathy. *PLoS One*, *14*(12), Article e0225964. https://doi.org/10.1371/journal.pone.0225964

Marmot, M. (2015). *The health gap: The challenge of an unequal world*. Bloomsbury.

Mashuri, A., & Zaduqisti, E. (2015). The effect of intergroup threat and social identity salience on belief in conspiracy theories over terrorism in Indonesia: Collective angst as a mediator. *International Journal of Psychological Research*, *8*, 24–35.

Mashuri, A., Zaduqisti, E., Sukmawati, F., Sakdiah, H., & Suharini, N. (2016). The role of identity subversion in structuring the effects of intergroup threats and negative emotions on belief in anti-West conspiracy theories in Indonesia. *Psychology and Developing Societies*, *28*, 1–28.

Mason, R. (2020). Boris Johnson reacted too slowly to COVID-19 says former scientific advisor. *The Guardian* (April 15). www.theguardian.com/politics/2020/apr/15/boris-johnson-reacted-too-slowly-to-COVID-19-says-ex-scientific-adviser?CMP=Share_iOSApp_Other

Matheson, K., & Anisman, H. (2012). Biological and psychosocial responses to discrimination. In J. Jetten, C. Haslam, & S. A. Haslam (Eds.), *The social cure: Identity, health and well-being* (pp. 133–153). Psychology Press.

McCann, S. J. H. (2008). Societal threat, authoritarianism, conservatism, and U.S. state death penalty sentencing (1977–2004). *Journal of Personality and Social Psychology*, *94*, 913–923.

McCulloch, D. (2020). Former union boss gets virus workforce gig. *The Canberra Times* (March 20). www.canberratimes.com.au/story/6689290/former-union-boss-gets-virus-workforce-gig/?cs=14264

McDaid, D., & Merkur, S. (2014). To nudge, or not to nudge, that is the question. *Eurohealth*, *20*, 3–5.

McElroy, J. (2020). Why B.C. is flattening the COVID-19 curve while numbers in central Canada surge. *Canadian Broadcasting Corporation* (April 6). www.cbc.ca/news/canada/british-columbia/bc-ontario-quebec-COVID-19-1.5524056

McKay, B. (2020). Lockdown blunder costs NZ Health Minister. *The Canberra Times* (April 7). www.canberratimes.com.au/story/6714105/lockdown-blunder-costs-nz-health-minister/?cs=14232

McPhail, C. (2017). *The myth of the madding crowd*. Routledge.

Meares, T. L. (2013). The good cop: Knowing the difference between lawful or effective policing and rightful policing (and why it matters) (program). *William & Mary Law School Scholarship Repository*. https://scholarship.law.wm.edu/wythe/11/

Memish, Z. A., Ahmed, Q. A., Schlagenhauf, P., Doumbia, S., & Khan, A. (2020). No time for dilemma: Mass gatherings must be suspended. *The Lancet*, *395*, 1191–1192.

Michie, S., Van Stralen, M. M., & West, R. (2011). The behaviour change wheel: A new method for characterising and designing behaviour change interventions. *Implementation Science*, *6*, Article 42.

Milgram S. (1974). *Obedience to authority: An experimental view*. Harper & Row.

Mills, S. (2020). Coronavirus: How the UK government is using behavioural science. *The Conversation* (March 25). https://theconversation.com/coronavirus-how-the-uk-government-is-using-behavioural-science-134097

Mols, F., Haslam, S. A., Jetten, J., & Steffens, N. K. (2015). Why a nudge is not enough: A social identity critique of governance by stealth. *European Journal of Political Research*, *54*, 81–98.

Monbiot, G. (2020). The horror films got it wrong. This virus has turned us into caring neighbours. *The Guardian* (March 31). www.theguardian.com/commentisfree/2020/mar/31/virus-neighbours-COVID-19?CMP=share_btn_tw

Moody, S. (2020). Games industry unites to promote World Health Organization messages against COVID-19. *Medium* (March 30). https://medium.com/@playaparttogether/games-industry-unites-to-promote-world-health-organiza tion-messages-against-COVID-19-launch-bfc6fc611641

Morton, T. A., Wilson, N. A., Haslam, C., Birney, M., Kingston, R., & McCloskey, L.-G. (2018). Activating and guiding the engagement of seniors through social media: Findings from the UK arm of the AGES 2.0 project. *Journal of Ageing and Health*, *30*, 27–51.

Moskalenko, S., McCauley, C., & Rozin, P. (2006). Group identification under conditions of threat: College students' attachment to country, family, ethnicity, religion, and university before and after September 11, 2001. *Political Psychology*, *27*, 77–97.

Moulding, R., Nix-Carnell, S., Schnabel, A., Nedeljkovic, M., Burnside, E. E., Lentini, A. F., & Mehzabin, N. (2016). Better the devil you know than a world you don't? Intolerance of uncertainty and worldview explanations for belief in conspiracy theories. *Personality and Individual Differences*, *98*, 345–354.

Muldoon, O. T., Acharya, K., Jay, S., Adhikari, K., Pettigrew, J., & Lowe, R. D. (2017). Community identity and collective efficacy: A social cure for traumatic stress in post-earthquake Nepal. *European Journal of Social Psychology*, *47*, 904–915.

Muldoon, O. T., Haslam, S. A., Haslam, C., Cruwys, T., Kearns, M., & Jetten, J. (2019). The social psychology of responses to trauma: Social identity pathways associated with divergent traumatic responses. *European Review of Social Psychology*, *30*, 311–348.

Murray, D. R., & Schaller, M. (2016). The behavioral immune system: Implications for social cognition, social interaction, and social influence. *Advances in Experimental Social Psychology*, *53*, 75–129.

Neal, M. (2020). Good Friday was Lifeline's busiest day ever as coronavirus puts strain on mental health. *ABC News* (April 19). www.abc.net.au/news/2020-04-19/good-friday-was-lifeline-busiest-day-ever-coronavirus-anxiety/12161104

Neville, F., Novelli, D., Drury, J., & Reicher, S. D. (in press). Shared social identity transforms social relations in imaginary crowds. *Group Processes & Intergroup Relations*.

Neville, F., & Reicher, S. D. (2018). Crowds, social identities and the shaping of everyday social relations. In C. J. Hewer & E. Lyons (Eds.), *Political psychology: A social psychological approach* (pp. 231–252). Wiley.

Noor, P. (2020). No masks allowed: Stores turn customers away in US culture war. *The Guardian* (May 22). www.theguardian.com/us-news/2020/may/22/us-stores-against-face-masks

Norris, F. H., & Kaniasty, K. (1996). Received and perceived social support in times of stress: A test of the social support deterioration deterrence model. *Journal of Personality and Social Psychology*, *71*, 498–511.

Novelli, D., Drury, J., & Reicher, S. (2010). Come together: Two studies concerning the impact of group relations on 'personal space'. *British Journal of Social Psychology*, *49*, 223–236.

Ntontis, E. (2018). Group processes in community responses to flooding: Implications for resilience and wellbeing. Doctoral thesis: University of Sussex. http://sro.sussex.ac.uk/id/eprint/79752/

Ntontis, E., Drury, J., Amlôt, R., Rubin, G. J., & Williams, R. (2019). What lies beyond social capital? The role of social psychology in building community resilience to climate change. *Traumatology*. Advance online publication. doi:10.1037/trm0000221

Ntontis, E., Drury, J., Amlôt, R., Rubin, G. J., & Williams, R. (2020). Endurance or decline of emergent groups following a flood disaster: Implications for community resilience. *International Journal of Disaster Risk Reduction*. doi:10.1016/j.ijdrr.2020.101493

Oakes, P. J., Haslam, S. A., & Turner, J. C. (1994). *Stereotyping and social reality*. Blackwell Publishing.

Office for National Statistics (2020). *Coronavirus and the social impacts on Great Britain*. April 30. www.ons.gov.uk/peoplepopulationandcommunity/ healthandsocialcare/healthandwellbeing/bulletins/coronavirusandthesocialim pactsongreatbritain/30april2020

Ogbunu, C. B. (2020). How social distancing became social justice. *Wired* (18 March). www.wired.com/story/opinion-how-social-distancing-became-social-justice/

Otago Daily Times (2020). PM: Stay home and save lives (25 March). www.odt. co.nz/star-news/star-national/pm-stay-home-and-save-lives

Outten, H. R., Schmitt, M. T., Miller, D. A., & Garcia, A. L. (2012). Feeling threatened about the future: Whites' emotional reactions to anticipated ethnic demographic changes. *Personality and Social Psychology Bulletin*, *38*, 14–25.

Owen, T. (2020). An anti-lockdown protest leader has now tested positive for COVID-19. *Vice* (28 April). www.vice.com/en_au/article/m7q8my/an-anti-lockdown-protest-leader-has-now-tested-positive-for-COVID-19

Paine, H. (2020). Supermarkets prepare for 'food riots'. *The Chronicle* (March 6). www.thechronicle.com.au/news/supermarkets-prepare-for-food-riots/39 61319/

Pandey, K., Stevenson, C., Shankar, S., Hopkins, N. P., & Reicher, S. D. (2013). Cold comfort at the Magh Mela: Social identity processes and physical hardship. *The British Journal of Social Psychology*, *53*, 675–690.

Paradies, Y., Ben, J., Denson, N., Elias, A., Priest, N., Pieterse, A., Gupta, A., Kelaher, M., & Gee, G. (2015). Racism as a determinant of health: A systematic review and meta-analysis. *PLoS ONE*, *10*, e0138511.

Pascoe, E. A., & Smart Richman, L. (2009). Perceived discrimination and health: A meta-analytic review. *Psychological Bulletin*, *135*, 531–554.

Pengelly, M. (2020). North Dakota governor on brink of tears as he decries 'mask shaming'. *The Guardian* (May 23). www.theguardian.com/us-news/2020/ may/23/north-dakota-governor-doug-burgum-tears-coronavirus-mask-shaming

Phillips, T. (2020). Brazil: Bolsonaro's defiance of distancing criticized by health minister. *The Guardian* (13 April 2020). www.theguardian.com/world/2020/ apr/13/brazil-bolsonaro-coronavirus-COVID-19-social-distancing

Platow, M. J., Haslam, S. A., Reicher, S. D., & Steffens, N. K. (2015). There is no leadership if no-one follows: Why leadership is necessarily a group process. *International Coaching Psychology Review*, *10*, 20–37.

Powell, A. (2020). South Africa comes together politically against coronavirus. *VOA* (March 18). www.voanews.com/science-health/coronavirus-outbreak/south-africa-comes-together-politically-against-coronavirus

Radburn, M., & Stott, C. (2019). The social psychological processes of 'procedural justice': Concepts, critiques and opportunities. *Criminology & Criminal Justice*, *19*, 421–438.

Ramenofsky, A. F., Wilbur, A. K., & Stone, A. C. (2003). Native American disease history: Past, present and future directions. *World Archaeology*, *35*, 241–257.

Ranse, J., Hutton, A., Keene, T., Lenson, S., Luther, M., Bost, N., Johnston, A. N. B., Crilly, J., Cannon, M., Jones, N., Hayes, C., & Burke, B. (2017). Health service impact from mass gatherings : A systematic literature review. *Prehospital and Disaster Medicine*, *32*, 71–77.

Rao, H., & Greve Insead, H. R. (2018). Disasters and community resilience: Spanish flu and the formation of retail cooperatives in Norway. *Academy of Management Journal*, *61*, 5–25.

Rapp, C. (2016). Moral opinion polarization and the erosion of trust. *Social Science Research*, *58*, 34–45.

Rathje, S. (2020). Will the Coronavirus bring us together or push us apart? *Psychology Today* (March 18). www.psychologytoday.com/us/blog/words-matter/202003/will-the-coronavirus-bring-us-together-or-push-us-apart

Reeves, R. V., & Rothwell, J. (2020). Class and COVID: How the less affluent face double risks. *Brookings* (March 27). www.brookings.edu/blog/up-front/2020/03/27/class-and-covid-how-the-less-affluent-face-double-risks/

Reicher, S. D. (1984). The St Pauls' riot: An explanation of the limits of crowd action in terms of a social identity model. *European Journal of Social Psychology*, *14*, 1–21.

Reicher, S. D. (1987). Crowd behaviour as social action. In J. C. Turner, M. A. Hogg, P. J. Oakes, S. D. Reicher, & M. S. Wetherell, *Rediscovering the social group: A self-categorization theory* (pp. 171–202). Blackwell.

Reicher, S. D. (1996). 'The Battle of Westminster': Developing the social identity model of crowd behaviour in order to explain the initiation and development of collective conflict. *European Journal of Social Psychology*, *26*, 115–134.

Reicher, S. D. (2001). The psychology of crowd dynamics. In M. A. Hogg & R. S. Tindale (Eds.), *Blackwell handbook of social psychology: Group processes* (pp. 182–208). Blackwell.

Reicher, S. D. (2020). Transparency is key in a crisis – so why isn't the British government being straight with us? *The Guardian* (May 13). www.

theguardian.com/commentisfree/2020/may/13/british-people-lockdown-coronavirus-crisis?CMP=share_btn_tw

Reicher, S. D., Drury, J., & Stott, C. (2020a). The truth about panic. *The Psychologist* (March 15). https://thepsychologist.bps.org.uk/truth-about-panic

Reicher, S. D., Drury, J., & Stott, C. (2020b). The two psychologies and Coronavirus. *The Psychologist* (April 1). https://thepsychologist.bps.org.uk/two-psychologies-and-coronavirus

Reicher, S. D., Haslam, S. A., & Hopkins, N. (2005). Social identity and the dynamics of leadership: Leaders and followers as collaborative agents in the transformation of social reality. *The Leadership Quarterly*, *16*, 547–568.

Reicher, S. D., Haslam, S. A., & Rath, R. (2008). Making a virtue of evil: A five-step social identity model of the development of collective hate. *Social and Personality Psychology Compass*, *2*, 1313–1344.

Reicher, S. D., Haslam, S. A., & Van Bavel, J. (2019). The road to Christchurch: A tale of two leaderships. *New Zealand Journal of Psychology*, *47*, 11–14.

Reicher, S. D., & Stott, C. (2011). *Mad mobs and Englishmen*. Robinson.

Reicher, S. D., & Stott, C. (2020). Policing the coronavirus outbreak: Processes and prospects for collective disorder. *Policing: A Journal of Policy and Practice*. Advance online publication. https://academic.oup.com/policing/advance-article/doi/10.1093/police/paaa014/5812788

Reicher, S. D., Templeton, A., Neville, F., Ferrari, L., & Drury, J. (2016). Core disgust is attenuated by ingroup relations. *Proceedings of the National Academy of Sciences*, *113*, 2631–2635.

Reininger, B. M., Rahbar, M. H., Lee, M., Chen, Z., Alam, S. R., Pope, J., & Adams, B. (2013). Social capital and disaster preparedness among low income Mexican Americans in a disaster prone area. *Social Science & Medicine*, *83*, 50–60.

Renwick, D. (2019). Organising on mute. In D. Bulley, J. Edkins, & N. El-Enany (Eds.), *After Grenfell: Violence, resistance and response* (pp. 19–48). Pluto Press.

Rev (2020). Australia PM Scott Morrison COVID-19 briefing transcript April 2. *Rev* (April 2). www.rev.com/blog/transcripts/australia-pm-scott-morrison-COVID-19-briefing-transcript-april-2

Rogers, K., Hauser, C., Yuhas, A., & Haberman, M. (2020). Trump's suggestion that disinfectants could be used to treat coronavirus prompts aggressive push-back. *New York Times* (April 24). www.nytimes.com/2020/04/24/us/politics/trump-inject-disinfectant-bleach-coronavirus.html

Rosch, E. (1978). Principles of categorization. In E. Rosch & B. B. Lloyd (Eds.), *Cognition and categorization* (pp. 27–48). Erlbaum.

Roy, A. (2020a). The pandemic is a portal. *The Financial Times* (April 4). www.ft.com/content/10d8f5e8-74eb-11ea-95fe-fcd274e920ca

Roy, E. A. (2020b). Ardern thanks nation as New Zealand adjusts to 'new normal' of COVID-19 lockdown. *The Guardian* (March 26). www.theguardian.com/world/2020/mar/26/ardern-thanks-nation-as-new-zealand-adjusts-to-new-normal-of-COVID-19-lockdown

Saeri, A. K., Cruwys, T., Barlow, F. K., Stronge, S., & Sibley, C. G. (2018). Social connectedness improves public mental health: Investigating bidirectional relationships in the New Zealand Attitudes and Values Survey. *Australian and New Zealand Journal of Psychiatry, 52*, 365–374.

Sahadeo, J. (2005). Epidemic and empire: Ethnicity, class, and 'civilization' in the 1892 Tashkent Cholera Riot. *Slavic Review, 64*, 117–139.

Salisbury, D., & Patel, C. (2020). The hurdles to developing a COVID-19 vaccine: Why international cooperation is needed. *Chatham House* (April 23). www.chathamhouse.org/expert/comment/hurdles-developing-COVID-19-vaccine-why-international-cooperation-needed

Sandy, M., & Milhorance, F. (2020). Brazil's President still insists the coronavirus is overblown: These governors are fighting back. *Time* (April 6). https://time.com/5816243/brazil-jair-bolsonaro-coronavirus-governors/

Sani, F. (2008). Schism in groups: A social psychological account. *Social and Personality Psychology Compass, 2*, 718–732.

Scanlan, Q. (2020). Partisanship in a pandemic: Democrats more concerned about virus than Republicans, but increasing concern for all: Polls. *ABC News* (March 27). https://abcnews.go.com/Politics/partisanship-pandemic-polling-shows-democrats-coronavirus-republicans-parties/story?id=69781489

Schaeffer, K. (2020). Far more Americans see 'very strong' partisan conflicts now than in the last two presidential election years. *Pew Research Center* (March 4). www.pewresearch.org/fact-tank/2020/03/04/far-more-americans-see-very-strong-partisan-conflicts-now-than-in-the-last-two-presidential-election-years/

Scheiber, N., & Conger, K. (2020). Strikes at Istacart and Amazon over coronavirus health concerns. *New York Times* (March 30). www.nytimes.com/2020/03/30/business/economy/coronavirus-instacart-amazon.html

Schmitt, M. T., Branscombe, N. R., Postmes, T., & Garcia, A. (2014). The consequences of perceived discrimination for psychological well-being: A meta-analytic review. *Psychological Bulletin, 140*, 921–948.

Schonfeld, D. J., & Demaria, T. (2015). Providing psychosocial support to children and families in the aftermath of disasters and crises. *Pediatrics, 136*, e1120–e1130.

Schubert, J. N., Stewart, P. A., & Curran, M. A. (2002). A defining presidential moment: 9/11 and the rally effect. *Political Psychology, 23*, 559–583.

Sherman, D. K., Hogg, M. A., & Maitner, A. T. (2009). Perceived polarization: Reconciling ingroup and intergroup perceptions under uncertainty. *Group Processes & Intergroup Relations*, *12*, 95–109.

Shimizu, K. (2020). 2019-nCoV, fake news, and racism. *The Lancet*, *395*, 685–686.

Skitka, L. J., Bauman, C. W., Aramovich, N. P., & Morgan, G. S. (2006). Confrontational and preventative policy responses to terrorism: Anger wants a fight and fear wants 'them' to go away. *Basic and Applied Social Psychology*, *28*, 375–384.

Slattery, D. (2020). 'You want to go to work? Go take a job as an essential worker': Cuomo pushes back on coronavirus protesters. *New York Daily News* (April 22). www.nydailynews.com/coronavirus/ny-coronavirus-cuomo-offers-advice-to-shutdown-protesters-job-20200422-3sbv26zfg5a4dm7i3rw6s-whd6q-story.html

Smith, J. R., & Louis, W. R. (2008). Do as we say and as we do: The interplay of descriptive and injunctive group norms in the attitude–behaviour relationship. *British Journal of Social Psychology*, *47*, 647–666.

Smith, M. (2020a). Brits split on changes to coronavirus lockdown measures. *YouGov* (May 11). https://yougov.co.uk/topics/health/articles-reports/2020/05/11/brits-split-changes-coronavirus-lockdown-measures

Smith, M. (2020b). Many more middle-class workers able to work from home than working-class workers. *YouGov* (May 13). https://yougov.co.uk/topics/economy/articles-reports/2020/05/13/most-middle-class-workers-are-working-home-full-ti?utm_source=twitter&utm_medium=website_article&utm_campaign=working_from_home_covid

Snowden, F. M. (1995). *Naples in the time of cholera, 1884–1911*. Cambridge University Press.

Sodha, S. (2020). Nudge theory is a poor substitute for hard science in matters of life and death. *Guardian* (April 26). www.theguardian.com/commentisfree/2020/apr/26/nudge-theory-is-a-poor-substitute-for-science-in-matters-of-life-or-death-coronavirus?CMP=Share_iOSApp_Other

Solnit, R. (2009). *A paradise built in hell: The extraordinary communities that arise in disaster*. Viking.

Solnit, R. (2020). 'The impossible has already happened': What coronavirus can teach us about hope. *The Guardian* (April 7). www.theguardian.com/world/2020/apr/07/what-coronavirus-can-teach-us-about-hope-rebecca-solnit

Spears, R., Doosje, B., & Ellemers, N. (1997). Self-stereotyping in the face of threats to group status and distinctiveness: The role of group identification. *Personality and Social Psychology Bulletin*, *23*, 538–553.

Stacey, K., & Pickard, J. (2020). Coronavirus pandemic boosts popularity of Trump and Johnson. *The Financial Times* (March 31). www.ft.com/content/c7f5a8bc-eb0e-45e5-a080-bbfd6d317def

Steffens, N. K., Cruwys, T., Haslam, C., Jetten, J., & Haslam, S. A. (2016). Social group memberships in retirement are associated with reduced risk of premature death: Evidence from a longitudinal cohort study. *BMJ Open*, *6*, e010164.

Steffens, N. K., & Haslam, S. A. (2013). Power through 'us': Leaders' use of we-referencing language predicts election victory. *PLoS ONE*, *8*, Article e77952.

Steffens, N. K., Haslam, S. A., Jetten, J., & Mols, F. (2018). Our followers are lions, theirs are sheep: How social identity shapes theories about followership and social influence. *Political Psychology*, *39*, 23–42.

Steffens, N. K., Haslam, S. A., Reicher, S. D., Platow, M. J., Fransen, K., Yang, J., Jetten, J., Ryan, M. K., Peters, K. O., & Boen, F. (2014). Leadership as social identity management: Introducing the Identity Leadership Inventory (ILI) to assess and validate a four-dimensional model. *The Leadership Quarterly*, *25*, 1001–1024.

Stephan, W. S., & Stephan, C. W. (2000). An integrated threat theory of prejudice. In S. Oskamp (Ed.), *Reducing prejudice and discrimination* (pp. 23–45). Lawrence Erlbaum.

Stewart, C. (2020). Trump and the politics of a pandemic. *The Australian* (March 27). www.theaustralian.com.au/commentary/coronavirus-trump-and-the-politics-of-a-pandemic/news-story/95d3cbf610c6ce494d55438d1fd40ffc

Stott, C., Ball, R., Drury, J., Neville, F., Reicher, S., Boardman, A., & Choudhury, S. (2018). The evolving normative dimensions of 'riot': Towards an elaborated social identity explanation. *European Journal of Social Psychology*, *48*, 834–849.

Stott, C., & Radburn, M. (2020). Understanding crowd conflict: Social context, psychology and policing. *Current Opinion in Psychology*, *35*, 76–80.

Stubley, P. (2020). Queen's speech: Monarch's coronavirus address to the nation in full. *The Independent* (April 6). www.independent.co.uk/news/uk/home-news/queens-speech-coronavirus-full-transcript-text-read-a9448531.html

Swami, V., Voracek, M., Stieger, S., Tran, U. S., & Furnham, A. (2014). Analytic thinking reduces belief in conspiracy theories. *Cognition*, *133*, 572–585.

Swire, B., Ecker, U. K. H., & Lewandowsky, S. (2017). The role of familiarity in correcting inaccurate information. *Journal of Experimental Psychology: Learning, Memory, and Cognition*. *43*, 1948–1961.

Tajfel, H. (1972). La catégorisation sociale (English trans.). In S. Moscovici (Ed.), *Introduction à la psychologie sociale* (Vol. 1, pp. 272–302). Larousse.

Tajfel, H., Billig, M. G., Bundy, R. F., & Flament, C. (1971). Social categorization and intergroup behaviour. *European Journal of Social Psychology*, *1*, 149–178.

Tajfel, H., & Turner, J. C. (1979). An integrative theory of intergroup conflict. In W. G. Austin & S. Worchel (Eds.), *The social psychology of intergroup relations* (pp. 33–48). Brooks/Cole.

Takaki, R. (2012). *Strangers from a different shore: A history of Asian Americans* (updated and revised). eBookIt.com.

Tam, J. S., Barbeschi, M., Shapovalova, N., Briand, S., Memish, Z. A., & Kieny, M.-P. (2012). Research agenda for mass gatherings: A call to action. *The Lancet: Infectious Diseases*, *12*, 231–239.

Tanis, M., & Postmes, T. (2005). A social identity approach to trust: Interpersonal perception, group membership and trusting behaviour. *European Journal of Social Psychology*, *35*, 413–424.

Taub, A. (2020). A new COVID-19 crisis: Domestic abuse rises worldwide. *New York Times* (April 6). www.nytimes.com/2020/04/06/world/coronavirus-domestic-violence.html

Tavernise, S., & Oppel, R. (2020). Spit on, yelled at, attacked: Chinese-Americans fear for their safety. *New York Times* (March 23). www.nytimes.com/2020/03/23/us/chinese-coronavirus-racist-attacks.html

Taylor, M. (2020). Music and encouragement from balconies around the world. *The Atlantic* (24 March). www.theatlantic.com/photo/2020/03/music-and-encouragement-from-balconies-around-world/608668/

Tekin Guven, S., & Drury, J. (2020). After Grenfell: Social identity, social solidarity, and social change. Unpublished manuscript: University of Sussex.

Thaler, R. H., & Sunstein, C. R. (2003). Libertarian paternalism. *American Economic Review*, *93*, 175–179.

Thaler, R. H., & Sunstein, C. R. (2009). *Nudge: Improving decisions about health, wealth, and happiness*. Penguin.

Thapar, K. (2020). Coronavirus lockdown: 'Food riots are a very real possibility', says Pronob Sen. *The Wire* (March 27). https://thewire.in/food/pronob-sen-karan-thapar-coronavirus-food-riots

The Economist (2020). How COVID-19 exacerbates inequality. *The Economist* (26 March). www.economist.com/britain/2020/03/26/how-COVID-19-exacerbates-inequality

The Guardian (2020). The Guardian view on pandemic secrecy: Wrong and counterproductive. *The Guardian* (May 15). www.theguardian.com/commentisfree/2020/may/14/the-guardian-view-on-pandemic-secrecy-wrong-and-counterproductive

The Lancet (2020). Reviving the US CDC. *The Lancet* (May 18). www.thelancet.com/journals/lancet/article/PIIS0140-6736(20)31140-5/fulltext

Thøgersen, J. (2008). Social norms and cooperation in real-life social dilemmas. *Journal of Economic Psychology*, *29*, 458–472.

Thompson, E. P. (1971). The moral economy of the English crowd in the eighteenth century. *Past & Present*, *50*, 76–136.

Tomazin, F. (2020). 'Tsunami' of cases as coronavirus spreads where social distancing is a privilege. *Sydney Morning Herald* (April 4). www.smh.com.au/national/tsunami-of-cases-as-coronavirus-spreads-where-social-distancing-is-a-privilege-20200403-p54gr0.html

Trinkner, R., Jackson, J., & Tyler, T. R. (2018). Bounded authority: Expanding 'appropriate' police behavior beyond procedural justice. *Law and Human Behavior*, *42*, 280–293.

Tu, J. (2020). How female Prime Ministers are leading in this time of crisis. *Women's Agenda* (18 March). https://womensagenda.com.au/latest/how-female-prime-ministers-are-leading-in-this-time-of-crisis/

Turner, J. C. (1982). Towards a redefinition of the social group. In H. Tajfel (Ed.), *Social identity and intergroup relations* (pp. 15–40). Cambridge University Press.

Turner, J. C. (1991). *Social influence*. Open University Press.

Turner, J. C., & Haslam, S. A. (2001). Social identity, organizations and leadership. In M. E. Turner (Ed.), *Groups at work: Advances in theory and research* (pp. 25–65). Erlbaum.

Turner, J. C., Hogg, M. A., Oakes, P. J., Reicher, S. D., & Wetherell, M. S. (1987). *Rediscovering the social group: A self-categorization theory*. Basil Blackwell.

Turner, J. C., Oakes, P. J., Haslam, S. A., & McGarty, C. (1994). Self and collective: Cognition and social context. *Personality and Social Psychology Bulletin*, *20*, 454–463.

Tversky, A., & Kahneman, D. (1973). Availability: A heuristic for judging frequency and probability. *Cognitive Psychology*, *5*, 207–232.

TVNZ (2020). Full speech: Prime Minister Jacinda Ardern's address to the nation. *1 News* (March 23). www.tvnz.co.nz/one-news/new-zealand/full-speech-prime-minister-jacinda-arderns-address-nation

Tyler, T. R. (2006). *Why people obey the law*. Princeton University Press.

Tyler, T. R. (2012). Legitimacy and compliance: The virtues of self-regulation. In A. Crawford & A. Hucklesby (Eds.), *Legitimacy and compliance in criminal justice* (pp. 8–28). Routledge.

Tyler, T. R., & Blader, S. L. (2003). The group engagement model: Procedural justice, social identity, and cooperative behavior. *Personality and Social Psychology Review*, *7*, 349–361.

Uhl-Bien, M., Riggio, R. E., Lowe, K. B., & Carsten, M. K. (2014). Followership theory: A review and research agenda. *The Leadership Quarterly*, *25*, 83–104.

UK Government (2020). Scientific Advisory Group for Emergencies (SAGE): Coronavirus (COVID-19) response. *UK Government* (April 17). www.gov. uk/government/groups/scientific-advisory-group-for-emergencies-sage-corona virus-COVID-19-response

Ulubasoglu, M. (2020). Natural disasters increase inequality: Recovery funding may make things worse. *The Conversation* (February 27). www.theconversa tion.com/natural-disasters-increase-inequality-recovery-funding-may-make-things-worse-131643

Unger, J. B., Kipke, M. D., De Rosa, C. J., Hyde, J., Ritt-Olson, A., & Montgomery, S. (2006). Needle-sharing among young IV drug users and their social network members: The influence of the injection partner's characteristics on HIV risk behavior. *Addictive Behaviors, 31*, 1607–1618.

United Nations (2020). Acts of kindness spread amid COVID-19 outbreak as UN acts to counter threat. www.un.org/en/coronavirus-disease-COVID-19/acts-solidarity-spread-amid-COVID-19-outbreak-un-continues-counter

United Nations Office for Disaster Risk Reduction (2015). Poverty and inequality. www.preventionweb.net/risk/poverty-inequality

Uscinski, J., Douglas, K., & Lewandowsky, S. (2017). Climate change conspiracy theories. *Oxford Research Encyclopedia of Climate Science* (September 26). https://oxfordre.com/climatescience/view/10.1093/acrefore/9780190228620.001.0001/acrefore-9780190228620-e-328

Valentino-DeVries, J., Lu, D., & Dance, G. J. X. (2020). Locating data says it all: Staying at home during Coronavirus is a luxury. *New York Times* (April 3). www.nytimes.com/interactive/2020/04/03/us/coronavirus-stay-home-rich-poor.html

Van Bavel, J. J. (2020). In a pandemic, political polarization could kill people. *The Washington Post* (March 23). www.washingtonpost.com/outlook/2020/03/23/coronavirus-polarization-political-exaggeration/

van Dick, R., Lemoine, J. E., Steffens, N. K., Kerschreiter, R., Akfirat, S. A., Avanzi, L., Dumont, K., Epitropaki, O., Fransen, K., Giessner, S., Gonzales, R., Kark, R., Lipponen, J., Markovits, Y., Monzani, L., Orosz, G., Pandey, D., Roland-Lévy, C., Schuh, S. C.,...& Haslam, S. A. (2018). Identity leadership going global: Validation of the Identity Leadership Inventory (ILI) across 20 countries. *Journal of Occupational and Organizational Psychology, 91*, 697–728.

van Dijke, W. (2020). Jan en Romy helpen als vrijwilliger corona te bestrijden. *RTL Nieuws* (6 May). www.rtlnieuws.nl/nieuws/nederland/artikel/5113416/vrijwilligers-corona-ziekenhuis-rode-kruis-helpen

van Leeuwen, H. (2020). Will COVID-19 turn post-Brexit Britain into a European welfare state? *Australian Financial Review* (March 22). www.afr.com/world/

europe/will-COVID-19-turn-post-brexit-britain-into-a-european-welfare-state-20200322-p54cla

van Prooijen, J.-W. (2017). Why education predicts decreased belief in conspiracy theories. *Applied Cognitive Psychology*, *31*, 50–58.

van Prooijen, J.-W. (2019). Belief in conspiracy theories: Gullibility or rational skepticism? In J. P. Forgas & R. F. Baumeister (Eds.), *The social psychology of gullibility: Fake news, conspiracy theories and irrational beliefs* (pp. 319–332). Taylor & Francis.

van Prooijen, J.-W., & Acker, M. (2015). The influence of control on belief in conspiracy theories: Conceptual and applied extensions. *Applied Cognitive Psychology*, *29*, 753–761.

van Prooijen, J.-W., Staman, J., & Krouwel, A. (2018). Increased conspiracy beliefs among ethnic and Muslim minorities. *Applied Cognitive Psychology*, *32*, 661–667.

van Prooijen, J.-W., & Van Vugt, M. (2018). Conspiracy theories: Evolved functions and psychological mechanisms. *Perspectives on Psychological Science*, *13*, 770–788.

Waldrop, T. (2020). Fearing coronavirus, Arizona man dies after taking a form of chloroquine used to treat aquariums. *CNN* (March 25). https://edition.cnn.com/2020/03/23/health/arizona-coronavirus-chloroquine-death/index.html

Walsh, R. S., Muldoon, O. T., Gallagher, S., & Fortune, D. G. (2015). Affiliative and 'self-as-doer' identities: Relationships between social identity, social support, and emotional status amongst survivors of acquired brain injury (ABI). *Neuropsychological Rehabilitation*, *25*, 555–573.

Weinglass, S. (2020). Behind PM-cited study showing Israel is safest place, a rabbit hole of weirdness. *The Times of Israel* (April 19). www.timesofisrael.com/behind-pm-cited-study-showing-israel-is-safest-place-a-rabbit-hole-of-weirdness/

Wenzel, M. (2004). An analysis of norm processes in tax compliance. *Journal of Economic Psychology*, *25*, 213–228.

Wenzel, M., Mummendey, A., & Waldzus, S. (2007). Superordinate identities and intergroup conflict: The ingroup projection model. *European Review of Social Psychology*, *18*, 331–372.

Wheaton, S., & de la Baume, M. (2020). Von der Leyen slams 'only for me' coronavirus response: European Commission chief hits out at member countries. *Politico* (March 26). www.politico.eu/article/von-der-leyen-slams-only-for-me-COVID-19-response/

Wherry, A. (2020). 'We are all in this together': Will Trudeau's actions match his words? *Canadian Broadcasting Corporation* (March 31). www.cbc.ca/news/politics/trudeau-pandemic-covid-coronavirus-media-*1*.5516383

Williams, R., & Drury, J. (2009). Psychosocial resilience and its influence on managing mass emergencies and disasters. *Psychiatry*, *8*, 293–296.

Williams, R., Kemp, V., Haslam, S. A., Haslam, C., Bhui, K. S., & Bailey, S. (Eds.). (2019). *Social scaffolding: Applying the lessons of contemporary social science to health and healthcare*. Cambridge University Press.

Wohl, M. J. A., & Branscombe, N. R. (2005). Forgiveness and collective guilt assignment to historical perpetrator groups depend on level of social category inclusiveness. *Journal of Personality and Social Psychology*, *88*, 288–303.

Wood, M. J., Douglas, K. M., & Sutton, R. M. (2012). Dead and alive: Beliefs in contradictory conspiracy theories. *Social Psychological and Personality Science*, *3*, 767–773.

Woodcock, A. (2020). UK reaching coronavirus peak with signs nation is flattening the curve, experts say. *Independent* (April 15). www.independent.co.uk/news/uk/politics/coronavirus-uk-peak-new-cases-lockdown-chris-whitty-latest-a9467356.html

World Health Organisation (2020). Media briefing on #COVID-19 with @DrTedros [Video file]. *(*April 20). www.pscp.tv/WHO/1lPKqVdbnkeGb

Yates, T. (2020). Why is the government relying on Nudge theory to fight coronavirus? *The Guardian* (March 13). www.theguardian.com/commentisfree/2020/mar/13/why-is-the-government-relying-on-nudge-theory-to-tackle-coronavirus

Yea, S. (2020). This is why Singapore's coronavirus cases are growing: A look inside the dismal living conditions of migrant workers. *The Conversation* (April 30). https://theconversation.com/this-is-why-singapores-coronavirus-cases-are-growing-a-look-inside-the-dismal-living-conditions-of-migrant-workers-136959

Yzerbyt, V., & Phalet, K. (2020). Maintaining lockdown and preparing an exit strategy: A view from social and behavioral sciences. *Association for Psychological Science* (April 16). www.psychologicalscience.org/publications/observer/obsonline/maintaining-lockdown-and-preparing-an-exit-strategy-a-view-from-social-and-behavioral-sciences.html

Zabollis-Roig, J. (2020). 4 senators are now under fire for selling major stock holdings as coronavirus spread across the US. *Business Insider* (March 20). https://markets.businessinsider.com/news/stocks/4-senators-stock-sell-burr-loeffler-inhofe-feinstein-coronavirus-market-2020-3-1029018164

Zagefka, H., & James, T. (2015). The psychology of charitable donations to disaster victims and beyond: The psychology of charitable donations. *Social Issues and Policy Review*, *9*, 155–192.

Zou, L. X., & Cheryan, S. (2017). Two axes of subordination: A new model of racial position. *Journal of Personality and Social Psychology*, *112*, 696–717.

Index

Printed in Great Britain
by Amazon